Thanks for
all you do!
Blessings,
Cheryl

PARENTS
WHO LOVE
TOO MUCH

PARENTS WHO LOVE TOO MUCH

How Good Parents Can Learn to Love
More Wisely and
Develop Children of Character

JANE NELSEN, ED.D
CHERYL ERWIN, M.A.

PRIMA PUBLISHING
3000 Lava Ridge Court • Roseville, California 95661
(800) 632-8676 • www.primalifestyles.com

PRIMA PUBLISHING and colophon are trademarks of Prima Communications Inc., registered with the United States Patent and Trademark Office.

Library of Congress Cataloging-in-Publication Data
Nelsen, Jane.
    Parents who love too much : how good parents can learn to love more wisely and develop children of character / Jane Nelsen, Cheryl Erwin.
      p.   cm.
    Includes index.
    ISBN 0-7615-2142-9
    1. Child rearing. 2. Parenting. I. Erwin, Cheryl. II. Title.
HQ769.E755 2000
649'.1—dc21   00-061117

00 01 02 03 HH 10 9 8 7 6 5 4 3 2 1
Printed in the United States of America

How to Order
Single copies may be ordered from Prima Publishing, 3000 Lava Ridge Court, Roseville, CA 95661; telephone (800) 632-8676, ext. 4444. Quantity discounts are also available. On your letterhead, include information concerning the intended use of the books and the number of books you wish to purchase.

Visit us online at www.primalifestyles.com

Contents

Introduction

If you were to ask the adults you know what they believe is most important in life, chances are good that you would hear the words "children" and "parenting" almost every time. Ask those same adults what they find most frustrating, and you're likely to get the same answer. Having a child sounds so simple when you're daydreaming about it, but the reality can be incredibly complicated.

Visit any family home in America. Sit down in a quiet corner and simply look around you. It won't take you long to discover whether this family includes children—the evidence is everywhere. You'll see toys, either neatly piled in a toy basket or scattered across the floor by energetic youngsters. At least one wall and several tabletops will be adorned by photographs of smiling young faces, and the refrigerator is likely to be covered with art projects, report cards, and the memorabilia of childhood.

If you look a little further, you may discover the children themselves. They come in all sorts of sizes, ages, abilities, and temperaments, but one thing is certain: despite the occasional struggles and frustrations, their parents love them very much. In fact, in most families the arrival of a child is a landmark event, something parents will remember in detail for the rest of their lives. And as those children grow and change, learn new things, and set off on their individual journeys through life, their parents will accumulate and cherish a storehouse of memories, stories they will tell each other, their children, and their children's children down through the years.

This is the ideal picture. Too often there are others—parents who are bewildered that their children don't appreciate all they have done for them; parents who are frustrated when their children demand more and get angry and resentful when their parents decide they are old enough to "fly" on their own. There are parents who don't understand why their children did not become more responsible and goal oriented "after all I taught them." And most bewildering, "Why didn't my children learn to be more considerate of others when we were so considerate of them?" Perhaps this is the problem.

American family life revolves around children. Although families come in many different configurations these days (and we as authors believe that each and every one has the potential to be wonderful), most parents have one thing in common: raising and living with children is both the most challenging and the most fulfilling thing they do. We know that you love your children; you wouldn't be reading this book if you didn't

CALVIN AND HOBBES © *Watterson. Reprinted with permission of*
UNIVERSAL PRESS SYNDICATE. All rights reserved.

care very much about them. But loving children doesn't
guarantee that any of us knows exactly what to do to
raise them well. Despite the avalanche of parenting resources, most loving parents occasionally feel confused,
overwhelmed, and downright puzzled about parenting
and about coping with the day-to-day upsets and problems life with children inevitably brings.

Loving and raising a child or two requires a great
deal of parents. Being a parent means being willing to
sacrifice time, resources, and energy to the cause. It
means digging deep and finding enough love to go

around. It means developing patience—rarely an easy task. It means learning to make good decisions, set boundaries, and guide children toward a happy, healthy life. And this is where many well-meaning, loving parents begin to worry.

As we will discover in the pages ahead, love is rarely the issue in raising children. Ask any parent who has watched the birth of an infant, played hide and seek with a giggling toddler, or watched a young adult head off into the world for the first time, and he or she will tell you how overwhelming that sense of love can feel. Parents love their children so much that they will do anything for them, sacrifice themselves for their welfare, go without the things they need to give children the things they want. They monitor behavior and food intake, provide fun and entertainment, push children to excel, and have high expectations, all in the name of love.

But is love enough? After all, parents do so many different things in the name of love. They control and they pamper, they give and they take away, and they punish and they hug, all in the name of love. (In fact, they may do it all in a single day!) A recent episode of the *Maury Povich* show featured mothers who had seriously obese babies and toddlers, some of whom weighed more than a hundred pounds at three years of age. Medical experts, an appalled audience, and Maury himself·asked these parents why they continued to feed their children everything they wanted in the face of overwhelming evidence that it was harmful to their emotional and physical health. One by one, these moms gave the same answer: "Because we love our kids." Many of these mothers had gone without the basics of life when they were young and depriving their children of anything they seemed to want, no matter how unhealthy, felt unloving to them.

Obviously, this case is an extreme example. But in a world where parents are more educated and more affluent than they have ever been before, why are we seeing such a shocking increase in violence among young people? Why do children so often seem disrespectful and selfish? What happened to old-fashioned gratitude and hard work? What is happening to our children? What sort of adults are they becoming?

The truth is that loving children as much as we do doesn't automatically produce effective, healthy parenting choices. In fact, love often leads well-intentioned parents to go to extremes. Parents usually are either too controlling and firm with their children ("for their own good") or too kind and permissive (wanting everyone to "feel good"). One parent was shocked when we suggested her eight-year-old child could make her own lunches and in the process could develop the belief that she was a capable, contributing member of the family—and that she was more likely to eat a lunch she fixed herself instead of throwing it in the trash. The parent said, "But I thought a loving parent was supposed to make her child's lunches."

Parents who love children too much usually do too much for them. Sometimes loving parents are too controlling about some aspects of their children's lives and permissive about others, and family life can easily degenerate into a series of power struggles, arguments, and hassles. We know this, incidentally, because we, too, are loving parents who have made our share of mistakes.

Every parent we have talked to in our workshops and on our travels wants to do a good job. Each one believes that raising a child is terribly important. But they are confused. Parents these days are overwhelmed with programs and approaches and often are guilt-stricken over their own conflicting feelings and needs (work or family?). And criticism is everywhere. Bookstore shelves overflow with manuals claiming to offer the best way to raise children. Radio and television experts abound. Magazines dedicated to parenting contain dozens of articles on discipline, few of which seem to say the same thing. Even the Internet is abuzz with parenting and family web sites, each offering its own take on the "best" way to raise your children. How are parents supposed to know what to do? Where does the truth lie? If excessive control and permissiveness aren't the answer (and, as you will see, we firmly believe that they are not), what is?

This book is not intended to give you "the" answer. It *is* intended to help you discover the answers that work for you and your children and to fulfill the dreams you have for them. The purpose of this book is to make you *think* and to encourage you to explore what you want for your children—which may not be the same as what your neighbors want for theirs. We want to guide you toward long-range thinking in parenting (more about that later) and to give you the confidence and skills to make choices for your children (and, as they grow and mature, *with* your children) that will help them become capable, competent, happy adults who can both enjoy and make a contribution to the world around them. We want you to develop both the knowledge and confidence to parent your children with love *and* wisdom—and to know that what "feels" best is often not what "is" the best thing you can do to help your children develop the characteristics and skills they need to be healthy, happy, contributing members of society.

Parenting, as you have undoubtedly already discovered, is not an easy task. This world of ours has changed so rapidly, and our skills and beliefs about raising children have not always kept pace. In the chapters ahead, we will explore the world of parenting. We will share with you the experiences of parents who have generously shared their stories with us over the years. We will offer you opportunities to examine what you do (and whether it's working), where you came from as a parent, and where you acquired your ideas about raising children. We will also offer you ways to know your children better, to discover what *they* think about life and what they are deciding about themselves and how to function in their world.

Most important, we will help you discover an approach to parenting that really works, one that we call "kind and firm parenting." We will show you how to use the deep and abiding love you feel for your children to guide them toward a life you—and especially they—can feel satisfied with. You will learn to parent your children, in a way that is uniquely your own, based on knowledge of the long-range results of what you do.

You have undoubtedly wondered whether you're doing the "right thing" as a parent. And we're willing to guess that you've had moments when you were pretty sure you weren't. Mistakes are part of the learning process, and we all make them. As authors and as parents ourselves, we approach this opportunity with humility and the greatest respect for those who devote so much of their time and energy to children. Settle down, grab yourself something to drink, and keep an open mind—some of your unquestioned beliefs about parenting are about to be challenged. But we believe the results will be worth it: healthy, capable, happy children and confident, optimistic parents. Let's begin.

CHAPTER I

Is It Really Possible to Love Too Much?

All parents love their children. They may define the word "love" in diffcrent ways and may have different ways of expressing what they feel, but the bond between parent and child is almost sacred. Books, art, music, and even advertising immortalize the precious moments of childhood. Most parents can tell you that they have spent long, wonderful moments gazing down into the crib of a sleeping infant, feeling the weight and joy of this new life and the responsibility it brings with it. Parents know, too, that they have a solemn obligation to protect and defend and to nurture and cherish their children, as well as an opportunity to laugh with and enjoy them and to treasure their every "first" experience: the first tooth, the first word, the first steps, the first day of school—right up to the first date, and, eventually (not *too* soon, we all hope), the first grandchild, when the cycle of parent-child love begins again for a new generation.

The seriousness with which parents accept this sacred commitment is evidenced in the abundance of resources devoted to raising children. Parents buy and read magazines and books; they attend classes; they share parenting and behavior problems in church lobbies, coffee shops, and Internet chat rooms. They devote an impressive portion of their time, energy, and resources to their children, often at the expense of their own interests. Why? Because they love their children.

> Love is not the problem; it is the choices parents make *in the name of love* that are at issue.

Love is a miracle; we know that. Each of us can remember moments in our lives when we felt truly loved (and if we can't, we often yearn for that experience). The moments when we feel that love for our own children are astonishing in their intensity. Human beings can never have enough love. Can they?

Many people are confused or offended by the possibility, as suggested by the title of this book, that parents can love "too much." Actually, love is not the problem; it is the choices parents make *in the name of love* that are at issue, particularly since the outcome of those choices usually is not evident until it may be too late to change them.

The time has come to encourage parents to examine their own assumptions and choices about raising children and to understand that what may seem at a given moment like the loving thing to do may not, in fact, *be* the most loving thing to do. It is not our intention to bash or blame parents; we both work with parents and (most important) are parents ourselves. We understand only too well how challenging the task can be. Our desire is to help parents become more aware of the long-range results of the choices they make in the name of love.

Loving Too Much Is Normal

If you are a normal parent, it is likely that you "love too much" to one degree or another. In fact, few, if any, parents (except, perhaps, pathologically ill individuals who are not capable of loving at all) have not engaged in loving their children too much. Take a moment and see if you recognize yourself in any of the following behaviors. (It's okay: we all do them.)

Overprotection

Overprotective parents fail to recognize when their children are capable and competent. They refuse to let their children climb to the top of the jungle gym, ride their bikes around the corner, or encounter situations where their feelings might be hurt. As children get older, overprotective parents try to prevent their children from making mistakes instead of seeing the value of mistakes as a learning process that builds strength and skills.

Keeping children safe is imperative, but overprotection may cause them to become timid and nervous about their own capabilities. Some children simply rebel against hovering parents, and this rebellion causes many power struggles. Overprotection consumes a huge amount of parental energy, and children usually prove to be ungrateful. They rarely appreciate the reasons for parents' overprotectiveness.

Rescuing

Parents who rescue frequently find themselves on their white charger, galloping to their child's school at 9:07 A.M. with forgotten homework (which the parents themselves may have completed because the child waited until the last minute) or a lunch from McDonald's (because the child forgot the lunch Mom so carefully packed).

Rescuing parents intercede with teachers over behavior problems or simply confiscate the stolen candy rather than having their child endure the agony of a return trip to the grocery store. They make the missed car insurance payment themselves, rather than following through with the agreement to take away their teenager's driving privileges. "They're just kids," these parents say. These parents eventually find themselves wondering why these same kids find it impossible to take responsibility for anything.

Permissiveness

Most of us have been told that permissiveness is bad for children. But it's just so much *easier* than having to enforce all those rules! Sometimes, too, parents believe that children deserve space to blossom and explore and that the word "no" will somehow stifle their creativity and self-esteem. These parents usually receive a rude awakening when they realize their children have not developed self-discipline, self-control, or concern for others. Parents feel hurt and offended when others do not want to be around their "spoiled brats."

Excessive Control

Excessive control is tricky; it often doesn't look like love at all. Lecturing, nagging, punishing, and making children's choices for them may not make you misty-eyed with emotion, but parents who do a lot of this can be heard saying things such as "I love you too much to let you become a delinquent." Once again, children often prove unappreciative and resort to resistance or sneakiness. Parents often choose excessive control because they think the only alternative is permissiveness. In fact, many options between these two extremes are possible and will be discussed throughout this book.

Giving in When Children Whine, Coax, Cry, or Throw Temper Tantrums

It's fun to give children the things they want and see their faces light up with joy. It's the whining and crying part that isn't fun. Many parents went without the things they wanted or needed when they were growing up and honestly want their children to have a better time of it than they had. Others just hate dealing with tantrums and public disapproval in the toy store or supermarket.

Either way, children, being human, learn to work the system, and more of the same inevitably follows.

Making Too Many Decisions for Your Children

Many parents make decisions for their children, saying that they are "protecting" their children from making mistakes. However, it is when children make their own mistakes that they have the opportunity to learn from them. It is tempting to tell a daughter, "No, don't waste all that time trying out for the cheerleading squad; you'll only get your feelings hurt," when parents are pretty sure she won't make it. But what might have happened if Thomas Edison's mom had worried about the damage to his self-esteem and persuaded him to give up that crazy lightbulb idea after forty or fifty failures?

Most parents are shocked by the suggestion that it might be better for their children to experience an F on a school paper rather than the nagging control of their parents. What is even worse for children is when parents do the paper for them. This does not mean we are advocating abandonment. Parents can be very encouraging by helping their children explore the consequences of their choices and what they learned from them in a supportive atmosphere.

Indulgence

Indulgent parents really believe that their children cannot handle going without brand-name jeans and sneakers, eating at McDonald's just about every night, and participating in the latest toy craze. Indulgent parents believe they are doing "the loving thing" by providing their children with a TV (and all the other latest technology) in their rooms.

These parents are also the most likely to be heard asking how they can get their kids to clean up their rooms (and the living room and the bathroom and the front yard) or why the kids expect an immediate replacement for every toy they break (and they break a lot of toys). What parents don't seem to realize is that if their children are indulged materially, it only follows that they think they should be indulged in every other way.

Unreasonable Expectations

These are the parents who sign up for the best schools before their children are born, buy a computer for their one-year-old, start a reading program at two by placing word cards on every item in the house, and sign Johnny up for golf at four because the golf course is a great place to make business deals. During the school years they try to get their children enrolled in gifted programs. They engage in endless power struggles over homework, believing their children will be failures in life if they don't excel in school, something that has been proven erroneous in many research studies (which will be discussed in later chapters). The children of these parents sometimes spend hours with therapists dealing with their hurt and depression because they believe that they were loved conditionally rather than encouraged to blossom in their own way. Some live their whole lives trying to live up to their parents' expectations, while others drop out and become couch potatoes in total rebellion.

Not Expecting Enough in the Area of Your Child's Contribution to the Family

Childhood should be a time of magic and fun, right? And kids never do chores and problem solving the right way anyway. Too many parents find it easier to "just do it themselves" than to engage in power struggles over chores. These parents are often exhausted and resentful. They might be surprised if they knew how discouraged their children feel. Of course children rebel when being commanded to do things that are not on their list of priorities. However, they are much more willing to cooperate when parents engage them in the problem-solving process, and they learn important life skills as well. Involvement begets ownership, connection, confidence, and cooperation. (We will expand on this point in later chapters.)

Praising Excessively Because Children Need High Self-Esteem

These parents find everything their children do "*won-derful*" and "*fab*ulous." They have "One Hundred Ways to Praise Your Child" posted conspicuously on the refrigerator because they have been told that praise builds self-esteem. They have also run out of wall space for framed children's artwork. They don't realize that excessive praise creates "approval junkies" instead of confident, creative young people.

Fighting Your Children's Battles for Them

These parents send friends home for not being nice to their child, tell Mr. Smith next door that his window was already cracked and the baseball barely touched it, and insist that if the geometry teacher were doing his job, their child wouldn't be flunking. Other adults and children scatter and hide when they see these parents coming. The children of these kinds of parents learn that they don't have to be accountable.

Allowing Children to "Rule" the Home

These parents always put the needs of their children above their own. They eat pizza because the children always want it, go to Disneyland every year because that's what the children want to do, and have never gone away for the weekend together because the children might miss them or cry. The parents feel cranky and resentful, but the children are happy. Isn't that what matters most? The disillusionment sets in when parents discover that their children aren't really happy after all. Instead of feeling gratitude, the children whine for more and have temper tantrums when things don't live up to their expectations.

Working Long Hours to Provide Material Wealth

All parents want their children to have a good life in a good neighborhood with good schools. And working parents do not damage their children, Dr. Laura's opinion notwithstanding. But hardworking parents who knock themselves out to provide a lifestyle for their children are sometimes bewildered to find that the time they do have to spend together doesn't meet anyone's expectations. Children and spouses often make the working parent feel guilty for the time spent "building a future," so in turn, he or she indulges the children to assuage guilt, a vicious cycle that does no one any long-term good.

Thinking They Know Who and What Their Children Should Become

These are the parents who bore colleagues and neighbors to tears with long recitations of their offspring's prowess in school or sports. Or who insist that little Jimmy is going to be a concert pianist when the whole neighborhood knows that Jimmy spends every spare moment tinkering with car engines. Does Father really know best? Are these parents trying to change petunias into roses? Do they really love their children for who they are—or only for the people they hope they will someday become?

Fighting for Custody of Children

Surely a loving parent has the right to custody of her child. But what if there is more than one loving, healthy parent? Some parents conduct custody battles for years while children walk tightropes between them. These parents never take the time to "get into their child's world" to understand the damage they are doing in the name of loving them.[1] Sometimes there is no "happily ever after" for these children.

Allowing Adult Children to Stay Indefinitely in Their Comfortable Nest

You mean loving too much doesn't end when children are 18? But it's hard to find a good job. Apartments are expensive. He won't eat right. According to recent data, more adult children over the age of 25 are living at home now than ever before in history (usually because they can't afford to live on their own in the manner to which they have become accustomed). It's a good thing these parents love their children—they're going to be together for quite a while!

If you can admit to any of these behaviors (and many of us can admit to most of them), you have indulged in loving too much and can understand why we believe that loving too much is simply part of the human condition—and of normal parenting. However, you also may have realized that it is not beneficial to children *in the long term*. In a nutshell, that is our definition of loving too much: *actions done in the name of love that are not beneficial to children.*

---

1. For more on this topic, see *For the Sake of the Children* by Kris Klein and Stephen Pew.

So, the good news is that you are normal. The best news is that you can do even better to prepare your children for success in today's world. Our definition of success is "happy, contributing members of society"—happy because they feel loved unconditionally while still learning the life skills that will give them courage, confidence, and capabilities to fulfill their dreams, not yours; contributing because they understand the importance of giving as well as taking in family, school, and community settings.

> Understanding the long-range results of what you do today will help you make choices that may feel "unloving" at the moment but that will benefit your children immensely.

Is Change Possible?

As long as you aren't seeking perfection, you can learn to love in ways that will "feel" more loving to your children and that will help you and your children achieve better results. "Better" does not mean perfect, however. For the very reasons you love too much (human emotions being a huge factor), you are likely to fall into the trap of loving too much over and over.

If loving too much is normal and you're likely to do it again, why read a book about it? Because awareness can help you avoid the "loving too much" trap more often and/or help you make amends when you fall into it. Again, we are not suggesting perfection. We are suggesting awareness and the skills necessary to correct mistakes when they are made. The courage to be imperfect, an oft-quoted statement by psychiatrist Rudolf Dreikurs, is one of the greatest gifts you can give yourself and your children. From your example, they can learn that it is okay to make mistakes, learn from them, and correct them whenever possible. Understanding the long-range results of what you do today will help you make choices that may feel "unloving" at the moment but that will benefit your children immensely.

Emotions

Have you ever seen a mother bird tending her nest? She patiently warms her eggs until they hatch, then devotes herself to nourishing her young. What would happen if the mother bird became emotional and failed to push her baby birds out of the nest at the appropriate time (which seems to be an instinctual act) because she was worried that her poor little darlings might "suffer"? Those little birds might start acting like some of our children who do not want to leave their comfortable nests. Instead of learning to fly and forage for worms themselves (becoming capable birds), these babies never get the chance to develop their wing muscles or their survival skills—just like some of our children. Why should they when they are fed, clothed, and provided with all the material things their little hearts desire—everything they have seen advertised in the media or have been told by their friends that they should have?

When Emotions Replace Common Sense

Emotions are an important key to understanding why parents love too much. Many of our children are failing to become capable adults because their parents follow their emotions instead of their common sense. Loving parents want to protect their children from emotional suffering. (And children may truly believe they are suffering if they can't have the latest toy or CD.) When parents rescue them from this suffering, they rob children of the opportunity to learn that they can deal with disappointments or, God forbid, that they could work hard (*really* suffer) to earn their hearts' desires.

This probably makes sense to you. So why is it so hard to accept and even respect the suffering your children will encounter (knowing it builds strength, character, and coping skills) instead of protecting them from it? Because you love your children too much.

Creating Weakness

You may have heard the story of the little boy who watched a butterfly struggling to emerge from its chrysalis. He felt sorry that the butterfly had to struggle and thought he would help by opening the chrysalis. The butterfly fluttered a few feet and then drifted to the ground and died because it did not have the muscle strength to keep flying—strength that would have been developed through its struggle to leave the chrysalis. This struggle to learn and grow is built into the life story of most of the animal kingdom for a very good reason. It is meant to be built into the human story as well.

How often do we take the role of the little boy and rescue our children from struggles that would help them build the strength they need to handle the even bigger struggles they will certainly encounter in their lives? And why do we do it?

> When parents rescue children from suffering, they rob children of the opportunity to learn that they can deal with disappointments.

These questions will be answered in greater detail in later chapters, but a simple answer for now is that even the most loving parents lack knowledge about the long-range effects of what they do.

Knowledge (and Lack Thereof) of Long-Range Results

The little boy would not have followed his emotions if he had understood that he was hurting rather than helping the butterfly. Much of what we do is due to lack of knowledge—another key to unlocking the mystery of loving too much. We don't know of any parents who would rescue, overprotect, or excessively control their children if they truly understood that they are doing more harm (in the name of love) than good.

We know that parents who "love too much" have very good intentions. However, they may not be aware that their loving intentions do not produce the results they hope for. Their children may be missing opportunities to learn to truly value themselves (instead of feeling loved only when they are pampered) and value others (instead of loving only those who are willing to pamper them). Too many parents do not realize that when they overprotect and/or rescue their children (to protect them from difficult situations and hurt feelings), they are leading their children to develop the belief that they are not capable, resilient problem solvers. When parents are excessively controlling, their children may be developing the belief that they can't do anything themselves or that they have to rebel to have any sense of self or personal power.

From One Extreme to the Other

Conventional wisdom usually includes only permissiveness or overprotection as symptoms of loving too much. However, parents may not be aware that when they are excessively controlling (in the name of love), their children may develop the belief that they are valued only if they are pleasing others or are living up to the expectations of others. As we have seen, there are many ways to love too much, and sometimes parents mix them all together, being permissive one moment and excessively controlling the next. Throw in materialism and it is a wonder our children develop any character at all.

Materialism

A new disease is plaguing the world today. It is called *affluenza.* Affluence has increased our tendency to love too much in the wrong ways. Many parents in past generations did not have the means to provide their children with too many things. One mother reported reading the Christmas chapter in *Little House on the Prairie* to her young son, who looked up at her in amazement. "They got an orange for Christmas?" he said. "And they were *happy?*" Affluenza creates another disease called "more, better, different." Count the times in a day that your children ask for (or obtain from their generous allowances) some material object. Many parents complain about the ingratitude of children who open piles of presents at a holiday event and then lament, "Is that all?" These parents usually fail to recognize that they are helping to create the very behavior they deplore.

> Too many parents do not realize that when they overprotect or rescue their children, they are leading their children to believe that they are not capable, resilient problem solvers.

Parents (who have a vague feeling that affluenza is not a healthy state) sometimes try telling their children, "I can't afford it," even when they can. Their children know this isn't true and take it as their clue to begin the "Oh yeah" campaign. They beg, plead, bargain, whine, sulk, or scream. Parents give in. Parents don't seem to know that is okay to say, "I *can* afford it because I have worked hard to achieve financial stability and have developed strength and character in the process. I love you too much to deprive you of the same opportunity." (This allows us to repeat that loving is not the problem when that love is translated into choices that help children develop strengths instead of weaknesses.)

Have you ever noticed that children know when you mean it and when you don't? If you say anything with conviction (kindly and firmly) and then follow through by not giving in, the "Oh yeah" campaigns will cease. It is okay to show a little empathy and express your faith in your child's ability to handle disappointment. That is the kindness part: "I know you are feeling frustrated and angry. I have faith in you to handle this and to figure out what to do about it." Saying what you mean, and meaning what you say, is the firmness part.

Possessiveness

When parents treat children as possessions, it is hard to know whether the motive is lack of knowledge about the effects their actions have on the child or whether it is just plain selfishness. Possessiveness is a good example of loving too much—doing harm in the name of love.

The movie *Saving Isaiah* provides an excellent example of a parent who is willing to tear her child apart in the name of love. While deeply addicted to drugs, the birth mother throws her child in a garbage dump. The child is rescued and subsequently adopted by a loving family. The birth mother later recovers and decides she wants her child (now four years old) back because "I'm his mother." A truly loving mother might have thought more about what would be best for her child. This mother eventually does, but not until she has caused her child excessive pain. (Although we believe that children should not automatically be rescued from the difficult events that occur in their lives, parents are never justified in inflicting traumatic pain on children.)

The birth mother wins a court battle and is given custody of "her" child. It is heart wrenching to watch as the little boy is torn from the arms of his adoptive mother. Isaiah screams and sobs until he falls asleep. He then goes into a deep depression for months (with occasional bursts of destructive anger, in one case knocking down chairs in a restaurant) before the birth mother realizes she has not done the best thing for her child. She finally loves him too much—this time in a healthy way—to continue inflicting misery on her child, and she returns him to his adoptive mother. The pure joy on the child's face as he runs to his adoptive mother almost makes up for the horrible scene in which he is torn from her arms. Then the adoptive parents have an opportunity to show healthy love: they agree to visitation rights for the birth mother, knowing that a child can love more than one adult.

Those of you have seen the movie know that we have not mentioned the fact that Isaiah was an African American child and that his adoptive parents were white. As far as we are concerned, that point is a political issue, and we hope for a world in which race truly has nothing to do with love and what is best for a child. An African American child raised with a white family (or a white child raised with an African American family) will undoubtedly encounter struggles (until the world changes) and, with loving support, will have the opportunity to develop strength in the process.

But that's Hollywood, right? *Saving Isaiah* provides an example that is beyond the realm of normal parenting. However, its extreme nature demonstrates the things that can be done to children in the name of love. And there are equally intense, if less dramatic, examples in every family court, where divorcing parents tear their children apart while claiming to love them.

Sharing Instead of Tearing Apart

Parents often fail to understand that it is infinitely easier for children to love many adults (parents, stepparents, grandparents, etc.) than to have to choose among them. Divorcing parents sometimes get caught up in their emotions and use their children to get even with their ex-spouse. Or they may lack knowledge about the effects that their actions have on their children. Sometimes they're just selfish. Such a parent might claim that he or she wants custody of children "because I love them."

Parents love their children too much when they can't see that they are doing "bad" while claiming to do "good." Unless safety, abuse, or neglect are factors, it is almost always better for children to have open access to *both* parents. As we will learn in later chapters, guilt over divorce, custody battles, or single parenting often leads parents to love too much by being permissive or overindulgent. Loving too much can be a difficult trap to climb out of no matter what sort of family you have.

There are many ways that normal, well-intentioned parents love too much. In this chapter we have given you a taste of what we mean by loving too much. In future chapters we will explore why it is harmful to children, why you do it, and what you can do instead. Parents can let their love motivate them to choose actions that are beneficial for their children, even when those actions may not feel loving at the moment. As we have said before, it is not loving too much that is the problem. The problem is loving too much in the wrong ways. All parents can learn to say, "I love you so much that I will not rush to rescue you and deprive you of the opportunity to learn how capable you are." Parents *can* love in ways that produce healthy, competent, resourceful children. This book will show you how.

CHAPTER 2

What Is the Harm in Loving Too Much?

It has been said that in today's world children need both roots and wings to be prepared for successful living. Very simply, your children may not develop the roots they need for stability and the wings they need to soar when they are loved too much. In this chapter (and throughout this book), we emphasize the importance of considering the long-range results of your actions—something most parents don't do.

Sometimes Parents Just Don't Think

Even the most loving, thoughtful parents have been known to react emotionally or out of habit (the authors have done considerable parenting "research" in just this way); parents just don't think about the long-range results of what they do, especially when they are toe-to-toe with a defiant youngster. A typical example is the way parents impose punitive time-out. They say something that sounds good but is probably unrealistic, such as "You go to your room and think about what you did!" When they stop to think about it, parents usually realize that this is a fairly ridiculous thing to say for a number of reasons. Not only is the child likely to be too upset to do this, but also it's highly unlikely that a parent can control what a child will think.

Parents would like their children to be thinking, "Thank you *so* much for giving me this terrific opportunity to think about the error of my ways and to realize that from now on I must behave better." It is more likely that the child is thinking, "I'll show you. You can make me sit here, but you can't make me do or think what you want me to."

We often invite parents to think about how they would feel and how they would respond if their spouse, friend, or colleague said, "You go to time-out and think about what you did." They laugh and say something similar to "Excuse *me!*" or "I don't *think* so." If children made these comments to their parents, they would be accused of "talking back." However, when you think about it, why would a child respond favorably to a situation that would certainly not be motivating to you?

At the other end of the spectrum are parents who protect their children from experiencing the frustration and pain of disappointment by giving in to their demands for candy in the grocery store or for a car "because everyone else has one." These parents hope their children are thinking, "Thanks for loving me so much that I will never have to suffer. I will be forever grateful and will make it up to you by being the best kid on the block." These are the same parents who later can't understand why their children forget about gratitude and only demand more. When parents think about it, they realize that their children do not develop survival and problem-solving skills when they are never given the opportunity to practice.

What Were They *Thinking?*

Most of us have had the experience of looking askance at another parent's decisions and wondering how on earth he or she could have been so foolish. In the aftermath of the Columbine High School shooting, an entire nation (and its most vocal element, the press) wondered out loud how the killers' parents could have missed the fact that their sons were building bombs and buying guns. But how many of us are truly in touch with our children? How many of us are connected enough, educated enough, and courageous enough to parent for the future?

The Harm of Materialism and Overindulgence

Every Christmas, advertising creates a shortage of the latest toy craze. In 1998, it was Furby; the year before, it was Tickle Me Elmo. Pokémon soon followed, and future Christmases will undoubtedly bring another "must have" toy. What do parents do? Anything they can to make sure their little darling is not deprived. Many have awakened before dawn to stand in line at a toy store with a limited supply or have paid ten times the retail price to scalpers who advertise on Internet auctions or in local newspapers.

In fact, the 1996 movie *Jingle All the Way* provides the perfect illustration of the "buy your child's love" philosophy. In the movie, Arnold Schwarzenegger plays a distant, workaholic dad who reconnects with his son by managing to obtain for him the toy of the season. To do so, he fights an all-out battle with an equally dedicated mailman and, in a twisted transformation only too typical of Hollywood, reunites with his son by actually *becoming* the toy. That this testament to commercialism should have become a popular holiday movie (a "family" movie, no less) speaks volumes about how our society has come to view parenting and what we believe children require to love and respect their parents.

Keeping the Long-Range Results in Mind

Parents need to stop to think about the long-range results of what they do. When parents are indulgent and satisfy every demand, what are they teaching their children? Here are some possibilities:

1. If you want it, you should have it—now.
2. Let materialism control your life.

3. Don't evaluate advertising and commercials. Just do whatever they suggest.
4. You can't deal with disappointment in life—and I'll make sure you don't have to.

When parents overindulge, children are not deprived of the toy, but they are deprived of an opportunity to learn valuable life lessons. When parents avoid overindulgence, children can learn the following:

1. What I feel is always okay, but what I do is not always okay. I can learn to feel what I feel and then to evaluate what should be done.
2. It is okay to want, but I don't "have" to have.
3. I can deal with disappointment. I may not like it, but I will survive.
4. When a goal is worth pursuing, I can help create a plan to achieve the goal that involves my participation: to save my allowance, to do odd jobs to earn money, and so on.
5. My parents will listen to me, but they won't indulge me.
6. My parents have faith in me to deal with life's problems and opportunities.
7. I am capable.

Healthy Loving Versus Overindulgence

Parents can help their children learn these important life lessons in several healthy ways. The first is reflective listening.

Reflective Listening

Reflective listening means to listen without fixing. Validate your child's feelings by reflecting back everything she says until she feels understood. You can avoid sounding like a parrot by reflecting the feelings you are hearing as well as the words.

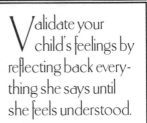

Validate your child's feelings by reflecting back everything she says until she feels understood.

Child: I want a Furby.

Parent (with a smile): You would really like to have a Furby. (You might be surprised how often this is enough, especially with younger children. The older children get, the longer the conversation might last.)

Child: Furby is so cute.

Parent: You really like this toy.

Child: Everyone is getting one.

Parent: You think all your friends will have one.

If reflective listening doesn't seem to be enough, you might try asking "what" and "how" questions. This can help your child enhance her thinking and problem-solving skills and can leave her with the belief "I am capable."

What, Why, and How Questions

What, why, and how questions are "curiosity questions" and should not be asked unless you are truly curious about what your child thinks (instead of using the questions to offer criticism or manipulate your child into thinking as you do). Your attitude and tone of voice are the keys to effectiveness with this parenting tool.

Child: I want a Furby.
Parent: Why do you want one? (Children are very suspicious of why questions unless they perceive that you are really interested in their answer.)
Child: Because they are cute and everyone is getting one.
Parent: How do you know that?
Child: I saw one on TV, and everyone is talking about them.
Parent: Lots of toys are cute. What do you think has made this one so special?

> Your attitude and tone of voice are the keys to effectiveness when using what, why, and how questions.

Child, after a pause to think about it: Maybe because of all the advertising, or maybe because everyone says they are so hard to find.
Parent: What is the purpose of advertising?
Child: To make people buy things. (Parent and child have had this particular conversation before.)
Parent: Can advertisers "make" people do things? Can they control people?
Child: They can't control me.

Of course, this conversation could go as many directions as there are children. One child we know concluded, "Last year Tickle Me Elmo was hard to find. Now they are lots cheaper. I think I'll wait 'til next year to get a Furby."

Brainstorming for Solutions That Involve the Child

Another child concluded the process of what and how questions with "They can't make me buy one, but I still want one." His father then engaged his son in a brainstorming session to help him figure out what he needed to do to get one. After brainstorming several possibilities, he decided he would find extra jobs to earn the money and then get his 23-year-old aunt to stand in a line with him. What do you think this child might learn about himself? About life? What would he learn if his loving parents simply handed him the toy?

It would not be helpful for a parent to say, "If you want this toy, get a job and buy it yourself." Brainstorming is effective only when the child is actively involved in the process and then chooses the suggestion that would work best for him.

Decide What You Will Do and What You Won't Do

Too many parents have forgotten how to use this very important tool. They feel guilty if they aren't willing to spend more than they can afford or feel guilty about saying no when they can afford it. In either case, they make the mistake of overindulgence. If you decide that buying a Furby isn't in your child's best interests, follow through with dignity and respect—without guilt. (It is often helpful to have a conversation with your child explaining your decision in a kind but unapologetic way.)

"But It's Easier to Give In . . ."

When you consider the negative long-range results, the harm in loving too much by overindulging becomes apparent. It is important to decide what you will and won't do and then to inform your children of your decisions kindly, firmly, and respectfully. If they feel angry or disappointed, use reflective listening to validate their feelings. This will probably be more uncomfortable for you than it is for your child!

It is usually easier for parents simply to buy the toy (and parents usually give in in the name of love). However, overindulgence is a very unloving thing to do to children. When parents overindulge their children, they are choosing their own ease over creating an opportunity to help their children learn important life skills and to develop self-confidence. The long-term results are not encouraging, for your children or for the people who will eventually share their lives.

> Brainstorming is effective only when the child is actively involved in the process and then chooses the suggestion that would work best for him.

Most American parents will confess that they have been known to overindulge their children with material things, even when it means parents must go without. But when children are raised permissively or overindulged, they are robbed of the opportunity to develop many important life skills, such as resilience, patience, concern for others, and problem-solving skills. They don't develop the courage and self-confidence that come from learning that they can survive disappointment and recover from mistakes on their own or, if punished or lectured for every mistake, from being allowed to learn from their mistakes in a supportive environment, without adult intervention.

When children are punished for or rescued from every mistake, they become less able (and less willing) to *learn* from their mistakes and may devote their considerable energy and creativity to defeating adults. How can children develop faith in themselves when their parents either protect them from all suffering and rescue them whenever they make poor choices or lecture and punish them for poor choices? How can they learn respect for self and others when they are not treated with respect? (Neither pampering nor punishment is respectful.) How can they figure out how to entertain themselves (or enjoy serenity) if their parents exhaust themselves ensuring that their poor little darlings don't suffer a moment of boredom? Parents who love too much don't think about these questions—or the answers.

Why Parents Don't Think

Parenting in our hectic world often has an urgency about it: it seems imperative to deal with each misbehavior, each crisis, each problem *right away*. Children have an impressive knack for frustrating, challenging, and angering their parents, but anger and frustration rarely prompt parents to do their best work. Thus, parents frequently find themselves *reacting*—doing what seems to work for the moment—instead of *acting* thoughtfully.

One of the biggest mistakes parents make is their failure—which often springs out of those impulsive reactions—to consider the long-range results of what they do. (We'll warn you now: you will hear this remark many times throughout this book.) What are children *really* thinking? What are they feeling? What are they deciding about themselves, about their parents, about life itself and how to live it? What behavior will these thoughts, feelings, and decisions produce in the future?

Example Is the Best Teacher

Parents want their children to "think" about what *they* do and to consider the long-range consequences of their

One of the biggest mistakes parents make is their failure to consider the long-range results of what they do.

actions, yet all too often, parents don't walk their own talk. For example, let's look at the long-range results of two perennially popular parenting styles (both of which are done in the name of love): permissiveness and excessive control. There are several long-range possibilities for each parenting style. We will look at these in greater depth in the chapters ahead, but consider a few of the possibilities.

Possible Long-Range Harm of Permissiveness
1. Pampered children who believe, "The world owes me a living"
2. Dependent children who believe, "Love means getting others to take care of me. I can't take care of myself"
3. Children who believe they are inadequate: "I'm not a capable person" (How could they decide otherwise if they have rarely had to solve a problem or learn the attitudes and skills required to recover from setbacks?)

Possible Long-Range Harm of Excessive Control
1. Rebellious children who decide that the only way to preserve their personal power is either to do the opposite of what is requested or to pretend they are complying while sneaking around to do what they want
2. Vengeful children who retaliate for the hurt and discouragement they feel and who often hurt themselves (by dropping out of school or other ultimately self-destructive acts) while trying to get even
3. Passive children—"approval junkies" who believe they are worthwhile only if someone else tells them they are

These are, of course, only a few possibilities. But if permissiveness and excessive control are symptoms of loving too much and you're still wondering, "What's the harm in that?" these "possibilities" can be sobering indeed. The fact is, no matter what form it takes, loving "too much" rarely produces the qualities in children that parents truly want them to have.

We have often said, "Beware of what works," meaning that what works for the moment may not have desirable long-range outcomes. For example, punishment may stop the behavior for the moment, and permissiveness may make the child very happy for the moment; but what are the *long-range* results for the child? What is the child thinking, feeling, and—most importantly— what is the child deciding to do in the future?

Children Are Always Making Decisions

Most parents don't realize that their children are always making decisions that affect their future behavior. Recent research on brain growth and early childhood development has taught us that despite the fact that they lack language with which to communicate, infants and young children are actively observing their surroundings; they are learning about moms, dads, babies, children, and what it takes to be loved and valued in their family. They go on making decisions as they grow and mature. These decisions form the foundation of personality and future behavior.

Children are not consciously aware of their decisions, but they are making them nonetheless. These life-shaping decisions often fit into the following categories:

- I am _____ (good or bad, capable or incapable, fearful or confident, and so on).
- Others are _____ (helpful or hurtful, nurturing or rejecting, encouraging or critical, and so on).
- The world is _____ (threatening or friendly, safe or scary, and so on).
- Therefore, I must _____ to survive or to thrive. (When children make decisions about thriving, they are developing into capable people. When they make decisions about surviving, adults usually call it misbehavior.)

Let's take a look at one of the most familiar examples of early childhood decisions. A three-year-old usually feels dethroned by the birth of a new baby. This child has had three years to be "queen of the castle." She has received unlimited love and attention, and she rather likes it this way. Suddenly, without consulting her, Mom and Dad bring home a baby. This baby is cute and she does like it (sort of), especially when she gets to hold it or play with it. But she also has become, quite suddenly, less important. Or so it seems. People come to the house, walk right by her, and coo over the baby's crib. They bring the baby presents. Worst of all, Mom and Dad are infatuated. They hover around the baby; Mom nurses it, Dad bounces it, and they talk about it all the time. She pouts and no one even *notices*. Obviously, something must be done about this situation.

The three-year-old observes all the time and attention Mom gives the new baby and *believes*, "Mom doesn't

love me as much as she loves that baby." The truth
doesn't matter; the child's behavior will be based on what
she believes to be true and the decisions she makes as a result. It is typical for young children who believe they
have been replaced by a new baby to act like babies; our
three-year-old friend loses interest in the potty, wants her
pacifier back, and insists on having milk in a bottle. She
also finds that she "can't" fall asleep without being
rocked and walked. This behavior makes sense to her and
is based on the unconscious belief that "Mom will give
me more time and attention if I act like the baby," but it
sure looks like misbehavior to Mom and Dad!

Perceptions and Decisions Are Unique

There are millions of possibilities about what beliefs
children will form and what decisions they will make—
as many possibilities as there are individuals. For example, one child may look at a tall, capable adult and decide, "I'm little, and others are big; I'll never be good
enough." Another child, looking at the same adult,
may decide, "I'm little now, but someday I'll grow up
and do even better."

> The truth doesn't matter; the child's behavior will be based on what *she* believes to be true and the decisions she makes as a result.

The point is that children
make decisions based on how they are treated by their
parents (as well as on other experiences in their lives).

Recent research indicates that children choose their peers (who undoubtedly have a powerful influence as they grow up) based on the values and beliefs they already have—values that were shaped at home by watching and learning from their parents (Ianotte et al, 1996; Glantz and Pickens, 1992; Pauman and Ennett, 1994). Different children can certainly make different decisions based on the same treatment, but many of their decisions will resemble those described earlier when children are pampered or treated with excessive control.

> Children make decisions based on their perceptions of what they need to do in response to how they are treated by their parents.

Getting into the Child's World

To help parents become more aware of the fact that children are always making decisions, we like to invite participants at our workshops to take the role of children. We ask them to take turns kneeling in front of a partner who is standing on a chair. The person standing on the chair (the "parent") then points a finger at the kneeling "child" while scolding and criticizing. At the end of the role-play, we ask them to share what they were thinking, feeling, and deciding while in the child's role.

Of course, the decisions vary. Some are feeling inadequate and decide they can never measure up. Some are thinking the adult is ridiculous and decide they will just lose respect and ignore the adult. Others are feeling angry and are deciding they will rebel or get even and are plotting how to do it, while some get so scared they just tune out. Most gain insights into the long-range effects of their behavior with their children, a new level of awareness they had never thought about before.

Thoughtful Parenting

Most adults would not consider embarking on a career (from bricklayer to brain surgeon), a hobby, or a sport without learning all they could and getting as much training as possible, yet they often shun parent education. We discuss the benefits and pitfalls of parenting education in chapter 5. For now, we want to emphasize how important it is for parents simply to think about what they hope to accomplish, who they want their children to become, and whether what they are doing is productive or counterproductive to achieving their goals.

We often encourage parents to trust their own inner wisdom. It is much easier to do so with confidence when you have educated yourself and understand that each parenting decision gives your children the right to make a decision in return and that those decisions do not always produce a respectful, self-reliant, motivated young person.

What Do You Want for Your Children?

Have you ever taken the time to make a list of the characteristics and skills your children need to be successful in life? What are the qualities you want them to have? We have had the opportunity to ask many parents from differing parts of the country, ethnic backgrounds, and income levels to consider this question: most come up with very similar lists. Here is a sample:

Characteristics and Skills for Success

Problem-solving skills	Respect for self and others
Compassion for others	Gratitude
Empathy and tolerance	Communication skills
Courage	Self-confidence
Integrity	A sense of humor
Love for life and learning	Responsibility
Resiliency	Kindness
Self-discipline and self-control	A moral and spiritual foundation

As you look at this list, consider the long-range results of your own parenting methods. Loving "too much" rarely produces the qualities that most parents tell us are important to their children's eventual happiness and success. Healthy loving, however, encourages children to develop these qualities and characteristics.

Conscious Irresponsibility

One of the best ways to help your children learn responsibility is for you to be "consciously irresponsible."

Parents sometimes spend endless energy and time being responsible *for* their children. They set their alarm clocks for them, shake them out of bed in the morning, issue incessant reminders to get dressed, eat breakfast, find their shoes, pack their bookbags, and grab their lunch—and still find themselves driving children to school because they missed the bus. It's a good system—for the kids (at least on the surface). But children aren't learning self-discipline and motivation (and often become discouraged about their own competence), and parents are becoming cranky, frustrated, and resentful.

> Children will not learn to be responsible when their loving parents are responsible *for* them.

What's the harm in loving too much? Children will not learn to be responsible when their loving parents are responsible *for* them. In other words, unhealthy love does not prepare children to be responsible, effective adults or happy, contributing members of society. (It's not particularly healthy for parents, either, who also deserve a little serenity, sanity, and respect.)

The Secret

There are many effective parenting tools other than the extremes of permissiveness and excessive control. It is important to mention that we are not advocating the other extreme—neglect. It is amazing how many parents are fearful that if they are not pampering or punishing, the only alternative is neglect. Neglect is never acceptable, but the big secret is that *many other alternatives are possible.* Over and over we hear, "I've tried everything." However, the "everything" these parents have tried usually falls under the headings of excessive control, punishment, permissiveness, or neglect.

Parents can empathize without rescuing. They can say, "This must be frustrating for you. What plans do you have to make things better?" They can be supportive while children learn from their mistakes and even help them explore the consequences of their choices instead of heaping on *more* consequences (which usually are thinly disguised punishment). They can express faith in their children to solve whatever problem they may be having and even offer to brainstorm "with" them if they are willing to put forth as much effort as their parents put forth. These are just a few of the many alternatives discussed throughout this book—alternatives that no longer need be a big secret.

> Parents can be supportive while children learn from their mistakes and even help them explore the consequences of their choices.

Parents occasionally find themselves swinging from one extreme to the other: they are permissive until they can't stand their kids, then controlling until they can't stand themselves. We will examine this phenomenon in later chapters; we will also learn more about discovering the balance that creates healthy loving.

Parents Who Love Too Much	Parents Who Love in Healthy Ways
See children as possessions	See children as gifts
Try to mold children into what they want	Nurture children to be who they are
Wimpy friend (or insist that a parent can't be a friend)	Respectful and supportive friend
Give in or make child give in	Kind and firm
Control	Guide (copilot instead of pilot)
Try for perfection (in child and self)	Teach that mistakes are opportunities to learn
Try to win over child	Try to win child over
Lecture or punish (for your own good)	Involve child in solutions
Treat as object or recipient	Treat as asset
Overprotect	Offer appropriate supervision
Avoid feelings (try to prevent or rescue)	Allow feelings and empathize
Fix	Teach life skills
Bawl out and then bail out	Allow child to experience and then *explore* consequences
Take behavior personally	Help child learn from behavior
Fulfill owns needs (mischief)	Get into child's world
Fear	Faith
Child centered	Child involved

What About Self-Esteem?

Many parenting books provide false notions about self-esteem. Parents are told they can "give" their children self-esteem and that they should be careful about damaging their children's self-esteem.

The most dangerous myths are those that have threads of truth. Self-esteem is one of those nebulous states of mind that seems to come and go. Have you noticed that there are days when your "self-esteem" is really good? You feel good about yourself and your abilities. Then someone criticizes you or you make a mistake, and your self-esteem thermometer drops to zero. Self-esteem *can't* be a permanent state of mind when a "bad hair day" can put such a dent in it!

> Parents who engage in healthy loving are more concerned about helping their children develop skills that will help them handle the ups and downs of life.

When scrutinized, the notion of being able to give children self-esteem doesn't make sense. Parents who love too much are often too concerned about a child's self-esteem, whereas parents who engage in healthy loving are more concerned about helping their children develop skills that will allow them to handle the inevitable ups and downs of life.

You now have several examples of what "loving too much" looks like, and we haven't even discussed guilt yet. (Guilt requires a whole chapter—chapter 6.) Many more examples are woven throughout this book, along with tools for showing love in healthy ways.

Is Your Love Hurting or Helping Your Child?

When all is said and done, this is the fundamental question we are asking parents to consider. You undoubtedly love your children and are concerned about their future, their success, and the problems they may face. This book invites you to think about what you are doing, why you are doing it, and the long-range results of what you are doing. You will also find many suggestions for kind and firm methods for healthy loving—loving from your heart *and* your inner wisdom—once you understand the dangers of loving too much.

Perhaps the most important message of this book is the importance of long-range parenting. Remember the list of qualities we discussed, those you wanted your children to have as adults? The goal of parenting—and its greatest challenge—is handling each day's problems and crises in ways that promote those qualities. Parents must always be *thinking,* "What will my child decide if I do this?" "What will he learn—about himself, about me, about what 'works'?" "What are the long-term consequences of giving too much, controlling too much, loving too much?" And in a world where parents feel torn between work and home, where they often feel they have too little time and too little energy, this sort of *thinking* is hard to do. Yet it is crucial that we learn.

In the chapters to come, we explore further what healthy love looks like and how to offer it to your children. You will learn what children need to be successful, capable, happy adults and how to approach discipline—which simply means "teaching" your children—in ways that nurture the qualities you want your children to have. You will discover solutions, ideas, and concrete skills that you can use.

> The goal of parenting is handling each day's problems and crises in ways that promote those qualities you want your children to have as adults.

But the most important part of the process is your willingness to look inside, to consider carefully and honestly the impact of your own decisions and beliefs about parenting, and to be willing to change the unhealthy loving that isn't accomplishing these long-range goals. Raising capable, confident, loving children takes time, energy, and patience, but it is possible. Be open to new ideas, trust your inner wisdom, and see what you discover.

CHAPTER 3

The Extremes of Loving Too Much

Permissiveness and Excessive Control

P arents rarely think of themselves as "extreme." You might ask, "How can it be extreme when I'm only doing my job? When I'm doing what I think is best for my child?" On the other hand, you may admit, "I know that what I'm doing isn't effective. I just don't know what else to do. I can't just let my child get away with this behavior."

As we've already discovered, considering the long-range results of your momentary parenting decisions is hard to do, particularly when you're frustrated by your child's behavior or anxious about his or her poor (and sometimes dangerous) choices. You do what you do because you love your child. Still, most parenting mistakes are made in the name of love. And many parents fail to recognize the extremes in their own parenting methods because they are flip-flopping between them so often that it *feels* balanced.

In chapter 1, we provided brief examples of what it means to love too much. In chapter 2, we presented brief examples of the harm that loving too much can do. In this and the next chapter, we take a closer look at the two extreme parenting methods parents choose (either excessive control or permissiveness) in their efforts to be "good" parents. Maria shares the dilemma of many others: "I'm permissive until I can't stand my kids," she says, "and then I get controlling until I can't stand myself. Even though I love my children very much, parenting isn't much fun with either extreme. I just don't know what else to do." There's that old refrain again: "I just don't know what else to do." This seems to epitomize the dilemma of parents who love too much.

The Dilemma

Just about everyone we talk to is appalled by the examples they see of children who demand instant gratification—"I want it now!"—and who have temper tantrums until their parents give in. These people are disgusted by the many examples they see of teenagers who destroy the property of others, just for the "fun" of it. We can all, unfortunately, tell stories of teens and preteens (and even younger children) who bash mailboxes, egg homes, run their cars over front lawns, smash Christmas lights, and so on. You are undoubtedly familiar with too many children who are unpleasant to be around because they are rude, demanding, thoughtless, and selfish. Surely you have heard comments (or have made them yourself) about how sad it is to see children "run the household." Everyone is talking about these kids and about the sad state of the society that produces such children, but who or what is responsible? Most people think it is plain common sense that children need more discipline, which is where the confusion and the problems begin: What *is* discipline?

Discipline and Punishment Are Not the Same

Most people in our society believe that discipline and punishment are the same thing, but they are not. Some parents think the most loving thing they can do is to "teach" their children through punishment. After all, they don't want to be accused of letting their children run wild or turn into one of the unpleasant creatures described a few paragraphs ago. To combat this possibility, parents become excessively controlling.

Other parents think the most loving thing they can do is spare their children from the humiliation of punishment. After all, they don't want to give their children examples of violence or the misuse of power and control. These parents often become too permissive. And, of course, many vacillate between the two extremes.

The Big Secret

The "big" secret was revealed in chapter 2 and is emphasized again here. There *is* something between the two extremes. It is called kindness and firmness at the same time, and it does not involve excessive control, punishment, or permissiveness. It *does* involve true discipline: teaching children appropriate behavior, good judgment, personal accountability, and the attitudes and perceptions that enable human beings to do their best in life.

Parents are most effective when they provide children with the kind of discipline that has nothing to do with the extremes. Children need the kind of discipline that teaches them self-discipline

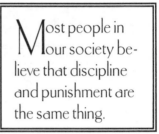

Most people in our society believe that discipline and punishment are the same thing.

rather than the need for external control. They need the kind of discipline that teaches them important life skills, such as respectful communication and problem-solving skills. They need the kind of discipline that teaches them concern and respect for others as well as for themselves. In other words, they need the kind of discipline that considers long-range results instead of short-term fixes. We will provide many examples of what effective discipline looks like, but first we want to make sure you understand what is *not* effective.

Permissiveness: Why Pampering Is Disrespectful

Alfred Adler, one of the pioneers in the field of family therapy, taught that children can have three potential problems in life: (1) a disability, (2) pampering, and

(3) neglect. Adler went on to say that it isn't a physical disability that presents a real problem but the fact that most children who are physically challenged are either pampered or neglected as a result.

As a wise person once said, children learn what they live. If parents' actions teach a child "You are the most important person in this family; you should never be unhappy," that child is likely to become an adult who believes

Children need the kind of discipline that considers long-range results instead of short-term fixes.

the same thing and expects constant attention and service from others. If parents respect and care for themselves and each other, children have the opportunity to learn both self-respect and respect for others' needs and wishes, obviously an important part of becoming a healthy adult. The problem is that loving too much usually "feels" better to parents. Setting limits, saying no, and spending time caring for oneself (and one's partner) make too many parents feel selfish or unloving and require that they spend time they may not believe they have teaching children to entertain themselves—and so they choose not to do it. The long-term results are not attractive, as anyone who has married one of these self-centered individuals can tell you.

Excessive Control: The Other Extreme

Others have come to believe that excessive control is the answer. These parents rally against pampering and permissiveness and go to the other extreme of loving too much. They operate under the misguided belief that good, attentive parents can and should prevent their children from making any mistakes. They believe they can mold children into who or what they should be by setting strict limits and by using punishment to whip their children into shape.

Permissiveness and excessive control are widespread and represent the polar extremes on the continuum of loving too much. Why do "good parents" so often choose these extreme approaches in the name of love? As Ron Taffel noted in a *McCall's* article in March 1993, during the past fifty years the mental health establishment hasn't helped parents make wise choices or feel confident about their abilities. A review of ten major psychology journals concluded that not one article described a mother-child relationship as being simply "healthy"; Mom was inevitably seen as either too involved or neglectful. In

> If parents respect and care for themselves and each other, children have the opportunity to learn both self-respect and respect for others' needs and wishes.

fact, it wasn't long ago that "experts" blamed conditions like autism and schizophrenia—conditions we now know are primarily genetic in origin—on bad parenting (specifically, the experts being largely male, on bad mothering). Conscientious, concerned parents often wind up parenting to avoid mistakes rather than to teach and encourage. Insecure, doubtful parents find it astonishingly easy to feel at the mercy of their offspring or to spend their time in misguided attempts to shape every aspect of their child's beliefs and behavior.

Rudolf Dreikurs taught that the secret to healthy parenting—parenting that is respectful, encouraging, and effective—is kindness and firmness at the same time. Kindness shows respect for the child, and firmness shows respect for what needs to be done. This makes a great deal of sense, doesn't it? Then why is it so difficult to do? Maria (who just didn't know what else to do) says, "When I'm upset, I don't feel like being kind. And when I'm being kind, I usually forget to be firm. They

ROSE IS ROSE © UFS. *Reprinted by Permission.*

just don't seem to go together." This is precisely why so many parents are having problems. They don't make the effort to be both kind and firm at the same time, or they don't have the skills for discipline that include kindness and firmness at the same time. They have no idea what this approach would look like in practical application. (Don't you *have* to lower your eyebrows and raise your voice to be firm?) We will discuss ways to practice kindness and firmness at the same time throughout this book. First, though, let's take a look at the extremes that are so normal (although ineffective) for parents who love their children very much.

The Good Intentions of Excessive Control

Parents become controlling over the most amazing things. Consider the story of Janet and her daughter, Marian. Marian is 15 and undeniably mouthy and defiant. She is frequently tardy for class and disrespectful to her teachers, and she struggles academically. To her credit, Marian admits that she needs to remedy her school situation; she just complains that school is so *boring* and the teachers "don't like" her. She uses much harsher words to describe her mother.

> Kindness shows respect for the child, and firmness shows respect for what needs to be done.

Janet worries that Marian is going to get into serious trouble. She suspects that her daughter may be smoking marijuana with her friends.

Janet also is appalled and affronted by Marian's deliberate disobedience of her mother's rules about telephone and television use and her outright disrespect (when Janet and Marian get into screaming matches, which they frequently do, Marian has been known to call her mother a "f—— bitch"). Janet has installed locks on the doors to all rooms that have telephones or TVs, as well as her own bedroom and bathroom, but the last straw turned out to be an ordinary lightbulb. Janet's "consequence" for her daughter's "forgetting" to turn off lights is not to replace the bulbs, which means that the only rooms Marian is allowed into have no light. Marian's behavior is getting more reckless and defiant, despite her mother's strict rules.

Gordon is a frustrated stepfather; he and his ten-year-old stepdaughter, Amanda, argue on a nightly basis. One night he found himself chasing her through their house, both of them shouting angrily. Gordon freely admits that he is controlling and rigid—it's in his blood, he claims, due to his Latin origins. The issue Amanda and Gordon fight about? Showers. She resists taking them, wastes hot water and shampoo, takes too long, and generally doesn't do things the way Gordon has demanded. When Gordon and his wife visited a parenting group for support, discussion turned up the fact that he was adhering to the same "shower schedule" instituted when the children were babies. So his stepdaughter *re*sists, while he *in*sists, to the point of sitting on the toilet, lecturing and supervising while she cries in the shower, an approach he recognizes is becoming impossible as Amanda reaches puberty.

Who Has the Problem, the Parent or the Child?

Interesting enough, both Marian and Amanda meet the diagnostic criteria for oppositional defiant disorder, an increasingly popular "diagnosis" in the mental health community for children who are argumentative, often lose their tempers, defy or refuse to comply with adult requests, blame others for their mistakes, and are touchy, irritable, resentful, or vindictive (American Psychiatric Association, *Diagnostic and Statistical Manual of Mental Disorders,* Fourth Edition, 1994). Although it is never acceptable for children to be rude, disrespectful, and defiant, Marian and Amanda's behavior was directly influenced by their parents' attempts at excessive control. Would their behavior change if their parents adopted a kind, firm approach to setting and following through on limits?

With the parenting group's help, Gordon and his wife decided on a different approach. They decided they would be happy with three showers a week and called a family meeting with all three children to invite their involvement in setting up a schedule. Amanda informed them that she preferred baths with music and a good book, and she was astonished when Gordon calmly agreed that she could take baths instead of showers, as long as she wasn't tying up the bathroom at a busy time. Gordon also did his best to ask for help and cooperation instead of issuing orders and to think about what his actions felt like to his children. It took time, and Gordon freely admitted that he made many, many mistakes. But gradually the yelling and arguing died down, and the entire family reported getting along much better.

As for Janet and Marian, they saw a therapist together for a while. Janet eventually admitted that she triggered some of Marian's behavior by making unreasonable rules and losing her own temper, but she was unable to give up her need to be in absolute control, and the screaming matches continued. After six months, Janet informed her daughter that she was no longer welcome at home. Marian is now in an outpatient drug treatment program and lives with her grandfather. She has not spoken to her mother in months.

Both Gordon and Janet are loving parents who believed they were acting in their children's best interests. How could things go so wrong? The truth is that excessively controlling parents frequently find themselves dealing with oppositional and defiant youngsters, children who have decided that the only way to keep their sense of personal power and self-respect is to defy their demanding parents. And defy them they do, despite criticism, harsh punishments, and grounding that goes on for weeks. A change in parenting style almost always produces a change in children's behavior—something the behavioral strategies and medications so often prescribed in these families rarely do.

"It's for Your Own Good"

Parents often insist on excessive control because they fear that their authority and standing as a parent will be compromised if they are not obeyed in all things. Other parents become controlling because they are desperately trying to prevent their children from making the same mistakes they made. Stella provides a familiar case study of a parent caught in the "fear of mistakes" trap.

When Stella was a teenager, she became very rebellious. She did poorly in school, got into drugs, became promiscuous, got pregnant, and eventually had an abortion. Stella is now a successful stockbroker. Even though she is a single parent, she has provided a lovely home in an excellent neighborhood for herself and her 14-year-old daughter, Jenny. However, she lives in constant fear that Jenny will make the mistakes she made and tries to prevent this through excessive control.

> A change in parenting style almost always produces a change in children's behavior.

Jenny does very well in school, yet her mother is constantly "on" her. Stella doesn't have faith in Jenny to care about her own progress. So, in the time-honored manner of teenagers everywhere, Jenny responds by failing to do her homework assignments until her mother nags. They have created the "I won't do it until you nag me" dance. Neither is very happy about the situation, but the homework does get done. It is easy to see why Stella might believe that Jenny will not do her homework without the nagging. Stella decided to drag Jenny to a counseling session with a therapist who specialized in parenting skills.

During the counseling session, the therapist asked Jenny, "How do you feel about your good grades?"

Jenny replied, "I like them."

The therapist then asked, "How do you feel about the nagging from your mother?"

Jenny said, "I hate it. Sometimes I don't want to do my homework just to make her mad, because she makes me mad."

Stella interrupted, "But you don't do it unless I nag. You wait 'til the last minute, and then you do sloppy work."

Jenny shrugged and looked sullen.

What would happen if Stella stopped nagging? We suspect Jenny's grades might go down for a while. After all, a pattern has been established, and any sort of change will feel uncomfortable for both Jenny and her mother. In fact, children often *escalate* their behavior to get the familiar parental responses— even though they complain about them. (Who said human behavior was rational?)

> Children often *escalate* their behavior to get the familiar parental responses, even though they complain about those same responses.

However, if Stella begins having faith in Jenny and helps her *explore* the consequences of her choices, Jenny is likely to become self-motivated. She has admitted that she likes getting good grades. Here's a tip that may sound irrational but is actually quite effective: If you want your children to be responsible, you need to be "consciously irresponsible." Being consciously irresponsible doesn't mean abandoning your child. It does mean that you become responsible for teaching your *child* to be responsible instead of taking over his or her responsibilities. Helping a child explore the consequences of her choices is one way to do this.

Exploring Consequences Instead of Imposing Consequences

Exploring consequences is much different from imposing consequences. Imposing a consequence might mean "No more phone privileges until you do your homework." Exploration happens when you wait for a friendly moment and ask questions that help your child think for herself: "What do you think caused you to get that lower grade? How do you feel about it? What are your goals for yourself? What ideas do you have to solve the problem?" A friendly tone of voice is essential. A threatening tone of voice invites[1] children to give the standard response: "I don't know." (Sound familiar?) Children can always tell when you are truly interested in what they think.

> Being consciously irresponsible means that you become responsible for teaching your *child* to be responsible instead of taking over his or her responsibilities.

---

1. We use the word "invites" instead of "makes" because your actions don't "make" your children do or say anything. Your children make their own decisions about how they will react to your actions. However, certain actions seem to "invite" similar reactions from most children.

After explaining this to Stella and Jenny, the therapist asked them whether they would be willing to stop their old dance and create a new one with the following steps:

1. Mom will not nag Jenny about her homework.
2. Jenny will be responsible for the consequences of her choices.
3. Mom will be supportive by helping Jenny explore the consequences of her choices—but only when they are both willing to have a loving and respectful conversation, and only to help Jenny figure out what she wants in her life and how to accomplish it.

Jenny thought this approach sounded great. Mom agreed reluctantly. Jenny, sensing her Mom's reluctance, said, "I'll tell on you if you don't do it." Everyone laughed, and the therapist clarified, "You may both need some outside support to learn new dance steps. I'll be happy to help."

But What About Drugs and Sex?

Of course, the homework issue was the easiest problem. Mom's fear of drugs and sex was creating the most misery—for both of them. When Jenny became interested in boys, as most 14-year-old girls do, Stella began panicking. Her fear led to more excessive control and, of course, more rebellion from Jenny.

The therapist requested a private session with Stella before tackling this one. She knew it would be necessary to help Stella discover where her fears were coming from and how they weren't helping her or her daughter. Jenny agreed to leave the room for a while. She grinned and said, "I'll work on my homework."

The therapist began their private session by asking, "In spite of your rebelliousness as an adolescent, how have you turned out?"

Stella had to admit, "Pretty well."

The therapist asked, "In fact, how has your past served you?"

Stella said, "Well, in lots of ways. I eventually became disgusted with my own behavior and decided to work hard to prove I wasn't a loser. I sought help through some wonderful spiritual organizations that have been very inspirational to me. In fact, I use these spiritual principles of love, forgiveness, and not being judgmental in every phase of my life—except with my daughter. Then I go totally into my fear." Stella paused. "Okay, I get it. I need to have faith in Jenny that it is her life to live and she has a right to learn from her own mistakes. I have been trying to control her because I love her, but I can see that isn't a very loving thing to do—and she hates me. It certainly isn't good for our relationship. But she wants to have *boys* in her bedroom! And there I go again."

Therapist: Do you really think she hates you?

Stella: No, but I think we both hate our relationship sometimes. That's why I'm here.

Therapist: What do you think she will do with the boys in her bedroom? Does she usually want to have one boy or more than one in her bedroom?

Stella: I'm afraid she will have sex, but it usually is a group of boys that come over. I don't really think she is going to have an orgy in her room.

Therapist: If she wanted to have sex, do you think it would stop her because she couldn't have boys in her room?

Stella: I know it wouldn't. My mom would never allow boys in my room, and I had sex anyway. But at least I wouldn't be condoning it. At least I wouldn't be a neglectful mother.

Therapist (smiling): So, which concerns you most, your daughter having sex, or you being a neglectful mother?

Stella: Both.

Therapist: So for now, it seems that the way to prevent her from having sex and to avoid being a neglectful mother is to forbid her to have boys in her room?

Stella: When you put it that way, I can see it is ridiculous, but I don't know what else to do.

Therapist: Would you be open to some other possibilities to help you achieve your goals?

Stella: Please!

Therapist: The problem now is that you see only two extremes: excessive control and neglect. The best path lies somewhere in the middle. How else do you think you could reduce the chances of your daughter having sex without being controlling or neglectful? Try thinking about what you wish your own mother had done.

Stella (sighing): I wish my mother had trusted me more. I know that a lot of my rebellion was to get even with her for not trusting me. It hurt, so I lived "down" to her expectations. Also, I felt so criticized by my mom; I couldn't do anything right. Oh, my goodness, Jenny said that to me just this week—that she didn't think she could do anything right. I can't stand it that I'm doing to Jenny the things I hated when my mom did them to me. I know that a lot of my sexual behavior was meant to find approval from someone. That was stupid, because who needs that kind of shallow approval? Oh, my gosh!

Therapist: You are having many insights about the relationship between you and your mother and how it affected you. Do you think your mother loved you?

Stella: I know she did. She just didn't know what else to do. And good grief, I'm doing everything I hated her for doing. No wonder Jenny acts like she hates me sometimes.

Therapist: Did you really hate your mother?

Stella: No. I loved her and I wanted her to love me—unconditionally. (Starting to cry.) Oh, I just want to go home and hug Jenny and tell her I'm sorry. I just want to love her unconditionally, and I want her to know it.

Therapist: You are moving very quickly with insight after insight. However, we aren't done yet. If all you do is love Jenny unconditionally, you might create your other fear—being neglectful. Sometimes unconditional love isn't enough. It is a great foundation—but children still need guidance. Can you handle a little more?

Stella: Give me a minute. I just want to feel how much I love Jenny for a little while. I have been too fearful and controlling to experience this.

Therapist: I'll go into the other room and get a cup of tea. Why don't you come get me when you are ready?

Stella sat and wept for a few minutes, but they were tears of joy. She was experiencing all of her spiritual feelings of love for her daughter now. It felt good and she wanted to savor the experience. After a few minutes she told the therapist she was ready—if she could have some tea herself.

Therapist: It is very moving to watch someone go through the profound transformation you just experienced. The next step will help you hold onto it. So let's go over your two goals. Actually, I think that your goal to avoid being a neglectful mother was just expanded to a much higher level—to show unconditional love. Now let's see what you can do to provide the kind of guidance that will decrease the chances that Jenny will become involved sexually. First, let's discuss the possibility that she might. What do you think it would mean to her and to you if she did have sex and even became pregnant?

Stella (thinking for a moment): We would both be fine. I would love her unconditionally and would help her get through it. I would support her in discovering how she wanted to handle it, and I would have faith in her to continue to live a good life.

Therapist: Wow. You are experiencing the wisdom that comes from unconditional love. So we have discussed the "worst-case" scenario and can see that it wouldn't be the end of the world. Now, let's focus on some skills that may decrease the chances that she will become sexually involved.

Stella: I have to admit that I'm not so worried about that anymore. I can't believe I was being so controlling instead of helping her learn to follow her own wisdom and to at least have safe sex if she does choose that route. Instead of having her focus on rebelling against my control, I'm going to have the kind of discussions with her that help her figure out what she wants in her life and to explore the consequences of her choices.

I want her to know that I will love her no matter what. I want to offer her advice, while making it clear to her that she can take it or leave it. You know, I have attended parenting classes and learned about this stuff. I just couldn't apply it when I was so scared. My fear blinded me to what is really important.

Therapist: Sounds good. You are way ahead of me. And I'm sure you've had the experience of feeling inspired and then losing it when you get out into the "real" world. Why don't we try a little role-play to give you some practice with the "dance" you have in your mind and heart. I'll be Jenny.

Making Changes Work

The therapist began to take Jenny's role. "Mom, I don't see why I can't have boys in my bedroom."

Stella responded, "I'm not sure I can see why you shouldn't, either. Would you mind if I ask you a few questions?"

Therapist: As Jenny, I'm thrown off by hearing you say you aren't sure why not either. I was all prepared for the old argument. I'm still suspicious. OK, "What kind of questions?"

Stella: Honey, I can see that you were prepared for the old battles, and I don't want to do that anymore. I want you to know that I love you unconditionally. That means I will love you no matter what. The questions I want to ask are questions that will help me understand what is important to you and may even help you understand yourself a little better. Is that okay?

Therapist/Jenny: I'm not sure how to deal with this. I loved hearing you tell me you love me unconditionally, but I'm not sure where this is going. I'm feeling pretty confused, like I'm hiking in uncharted territory. But I would say, "I guess so."

Stella: I have to admit that I have two concerns here. One is that I want you to know I love you and have faith in you. The other is that I don't want to be a permissive mother. I know I've been too controlling, so I don't want to go to the other extreme. Since we are both used to me being controlling and you being resentful of that, we have new territory to chart. Are you willing to work on a more respectful relationship where I can be the kind of mother who is caring and supportive without being controlling or permissive?

Therapist/Jenny: This is sounding too good to be true. It is also a little scary. I'm beginning to see that it will require more responsibility on my part. I'm still feeling a little wobbly. "Don't be so hard on yourself, Mom. You are fine."

Stella (with a big grin): Does that mean you would like me to keep being excessively controlling so we can continue our power struggles?

Therapist/Jenny (grinning back): Well, no.

Stella: Okay if I ask my questions?

Therapist/Jenny: Go for it, Mom.

Stella: What do you see happening in your room with the boys?

Therapist/Jenny (sounding a little disgusted): Well, Mom, we aren't going to be having sex, if that is what you are worried about.

Stella: Well, I was a little worried about that. It is reassuring to hear you say that. The truth is that I know that if you were going to have sex, you wouldn't need to use your room. So I guess the real question is, How do you feel about having sex?

Therapist/Jenny: Geeez, Mom. I'm not ready to have sex. Chill. We just want to hang out. We want a comfortable place to talk, without adults listening in. Not that we are saying anything bad. We just want some privacy. Is that okay with you?

Stella (responding lovingly to the defensiveness): Jenny, you may not believe this, but I was your age once. I can remember one day thinking I didn't want to have sex, and then all of a sudden it seemed like an intriguing idea. Frankly, I wish my mom had talked with me the way I want to talk with you. I'm not trying to invade your privacy. I just want to know you as a person—how you feel about things. I also want you to know that you can come to me for information and advice and that you can take it or leave it because you know I will love you no matter what.

Therapist/Jenny (suspiciously): Sure. (This is still sounding a little too good to be true. I just can't trust it yet.)

Stella: So, I think we have talked enough for now. I can tell you are having a little trouble believing that I'm really going to love you unconditionally. So how about this? You can have the boys in your room when I'm home. It is still not okay with me for you to have boys in the house when I'm not there, because even though I trust *you,* I don't know whether I can trust them. Anyway, when you do have boys in your room, I'll come knock on the door at some point and ask if I can come in. That way you can have your privacy, and I won't feel like a neglectful mother. Is that okay with you?

Therapist/Jenny: Sure. It might be a little embarrassing to have you knock on the door, but since we won't be doing anything we shouldn't be doing, it is no big deal.

Stella: I appreciate that. And I would like to talk with you every once in a while just to see how you are feeling about things. Oh, and Jenny, remember: I'm not going to nag you about your homework anymore. If you don't get it done, that will be between you and your teachers. I'm willing to help when you need it, but you will need to give me advance notice. I won't drop my plans for last-minute emergencies. Okay?

Therapist/Jenny: Okay. (Yikes! What am I going to do now that I have what I thought I always wanted?)

The therapist smiled. "Good job, Stella. I couldn't have done it any better."

Stella relaxed and smiled back. "I'll let you know how it goes."

This story has a funny sequel. Jenny was thrilled with the changes her mother made. She said, "I just love that counselor." However, the first day she had boys in her room, they accidentally knocked some of the decorations off her wall. She had spent hours placing them precisely and was not happy. She told her mom, "I think we'll just go in the den from now on."

> It is typical that once the battleground is turned into a peace field, children think more *for* themselves than *against* their parents.

It is typical that once the battleground is turned into a peace field, children think more *for* themselves than *against* their parents. This story makes several points:

1. Excessive control based on fear creates irrational behavior.
2. Control, in the name of love, smothers true love and creates power struggles.
3. Control usually creates the opposite of intended goals. Instead of motivating cooperation, it motivates rebellion.

4. Love is found when the clouds of fear are blown away through an understanding of the real issues.
5. Unconditional love inspires wisdom, which includes kindness and firmness at the same time.
6. Unconditional love and kind and firm guidance invite cooperation.

Stella's new approach to her daughter is not permissive. She has not abdicated her parental responsibility to set boundaries and supervise; she has merely stopped trying to control Jenny and begun a process of trust, teaching problem solving and good judgment—a process this mother and daughter will share for many years to come. Too many parents are fearful that if they stop being controlling, the only alternative is permissiveness. They certainly don't want that, and for good reason: Permissiveness is no healthier than excessive control. We explore the causes and effects of permissiveness in the next chapter.

Permissiveness
Good Intentions or by Default?

Why are parents permissive? In addition to the many reasons discussed in chapter 4 (such as wanting children to have happy childhoods), it is often just plain easier. Children hassle, hassle, hassle. Parents say no, no, no. Children hassle, hassle, hassle. Parents say no, no, no. Children hassle, hassle, hassle. Parents give in.

This scene is repeated over and over and over—in grocery stores, at the mall, during bedtime, in the morning. Just as excessive control invites children to think and act "against" their parents, permissiveness invites children to think and act "for" themselves in selfish ways. Permissiveness invites children to adopt the belief that "The world owes me a living" or "Love means getting other people to give me everything I want." When children hassle and parents eventually give in, parents teach their children that no doesn't mean no. It means "keep hassling until I give in."

Permissiveness and pampering go hand in hand, and parents do it because it seems to work at the moment. After all, most children do stop crying when they get their own way. Parents also claim they punish their children because the behavior stops—at least for the moment. In either case, parents are not considering the long-range results—the decisions their children are making and how they will affect future behavior.

"But I Would Never Do That . . ."

Permissiveness is almost always something *other* parents do, and most parents recognize its ineffectiveness when they see other parents doing it. Millions of people watched, appalled, as a film crew for a popular TV newsmagazine followed parents who took their two children to a large discount store. One child wanted a toy. The parents talked to him very kindly and reasonably about why he couldn't have the toy. The child had a temper tantrum. He grabbed the toy from the shelf and put it in the cart. The mother took it out of the cart and put it back on the shelf while continuing to discuss the matter very firmly. But as the child's decibel level increased, Mom's willpower decreased. Finally, she gave in and bought the toy for the child.

This caving in provoked a great deal of comment from viewers. Some said, "That kid should have received a spanking the minute he had a temper tantrum."

Others said, "I can't believe those parents could be so wimpy." Or, "I would certainly never let my child get away with that."

It is true that the parents were being wimpy "in the name of love." (And chances are that these parents would have been horrified themselves had they been watching someone else! It is very easy to judge others when you are not emotionally hooked and totally frustrated.) It is true that the children were not served well by having their parents give in to them. However, is the only alternative a spanking or some other form of punishment? Of course not. Neither method produces effective long-range results when you consider what children might be deciding in response to either permissiveness or punishment.

When children hassle and parents eventually give in, they teach their children that no doesn't mean no.

What were these parents thinking? We can only guess. Were they thinking, "I can't stand it when my child has a temper tantrum?" Were they concerned about what others were thinking? Or did they finally give in because they just didn't know what else to do? All of these thoughts probably buzzed through their brains, but the latter may have had the greatest weight. As mentioned earlier, many loving parents simply don't have any tools in their parenting "toolbox" other than permissiveness or punishment. It is likely that these parents did not accept the alternative of punishment and saw permissiveness as the only other option.

But there is good news: Many other effective options involve both kindness and firmness *at the same time.* As we have said before, kindness shows respect for the child, and firmness shows respect for the needs of the situation. What would parents who reacted to the previous situation with kindness and firmness act like? There are several possibilities:

Option 1: When the child asked for the toy, the parents could say no only once. Then they could shut their mouths and act. If the child engaged in a temper tantrum, one could kindly and firmly take the child to the car where he could have his feelings in private. (Later we talk about the importance of allowing children to have their feelings, which is not the same thing as allowing them to misbehave.) It is important to avoid conversation (children will use anything you say as fuel for an argument) except to say, "We'll go back to the store as soon as you are ready."

Option 2: When the child asked for a toy, the parents could ask, "Do you have enough money saved from your allowance?" When the child pouts and says no, they could say, "As soon as you have saved enough money, you can have the toy." (Some parents even offer to provide half. Most children do not want the toy badly enough to wait and save their money.)

Option 3: The parents could advise their children in advance that they will all leave the store immediately if there is any misbehavior. (Of course, it would be helpful if the parents had thoroughly described what misbehavior looks like during a family meeting and even allowed the children to learn by playing "let's pretend.") Parents could demonstrate appropriate behavior and what will happen when behavior is inappropriate. Then the parents could follow through and simply do what they promised.

Children learn very quickly whether their parents mean what they say. The child in this story obviously knew his parents didn't mean it when they told him he couldn't have the toy. To children, parents are a lot like slot machines: they don't always pay off, but the chance that they will makes it worth pulling the handle. When children know you mean what you say, they soon stop hassling.

> To children, parents are a lot like slot machines: they don't always pay off, but the chance that they will makes it worth pulling the handle.

Consider the long-range results of the television story and the three options. What did the child learn (and what decisions might he have made) when his parents gave in to him? What might children learn and decide after experiencing the other options presented?

There it is again—the importance of considering long-range results. Failing to do so is one of the biggest reasons parents love "too much." However, it isn't the only factor. Parents love too much for many reasons, some of them so subtly interwoven into our culture that they are difficult to spot.

Permissiveness, Laziness, Busyness, Bad Habits?

How much of permissiveness is really part of something else—our culture? When a parent allows children to eat junk food, buy designer clothes, and sit for hours in front of a television, what is this all about? It seems to be more than just permissiveness. We don't like to sound judgmental (after all, we have been there), but it is easier to pick up fast food than to cook a meal. It is easier to go along with the fashion trends foisted on us by the media (magazines, television, movies, music) than to follow common sense. (Actually, common sense is not so common these days.) Nothing can be foisted on us without our permission. It is easier to let the "boob tube" baby-sit our children. Is this simple laziness, or have we become victims (again, with our own permission) of a speeded-up society? Are we simply too busy? Have we fallen into bad habits? Whatever it is, it is not good for our children.

The Fast-Food Syndrome

Children scream for McDonald's, and parents give in. This is more than simple permissiveness. It is laziness. (Why cook when it is so easy to drive through?) Actually, when parents think about the long-range detriments of fast food, they will know why it is usually better to cook instead of driving through.

In the June 6, 2000, issue of *USA Today*, Greg Critser wrote an article on "Fast Food, Parents' Indulgence Conspire to Supersize Kids." Greg explains that *supersizing* is the term used to describe when a fast-food restaurant sells a kid 1,660 calories worth of largely fat and sugar for about 80 cents more than it would a similar meal of 1,300 calories. As a result, childhood obesity is now estimated at 11 to 15 percent of all American kids and threatening another 25 percent.

Obesity isn't the only problem. Many problems of fast-food diets may not be seen for years. It may take more than twenty-five years for a liver to be destroyed by processing so much sugar. Parents need to think about the long-range effects of eating 40 percent of their meals outside the home (or having pizza delivered), not only in terms of the effects on health but also in terms of what they are teaching their children.

Mr. and Mrs. Jolson decided that they wanted their children to have a different experience. In the Jolson family (Mom, Dad, Jill, Jeff, and Jeanie), every one cooks dinner once a week (the parents get double duty as there are five cooks and seven days in the week). Everyone has clean-up chores, and once a week they spend an hour really cleaning the house together.

Hannah, a 16-year-old cousin from another country, came to live with the Jolsons for five months. Before Hannah came, Mom wrote and warned her, "Our family is a little different. We all share the work in the family."

Mom wanted to warn Hannah so that she would know she would be part of the family and have family jobs, too.

When Hannah arrived, the kids decided that she should be a guest for a week and not have any jobs; that way she could see how things worked and get a little more comfortable. The second week the family held a family meeting to arrange the chore schedule to include Hannah. She reluctantly picked her night to cook and was very nervous. She did not know what or how to cook. Her parents had "loved her too much" to require her to do anything that would allow her to be a contributing member of the family. She did not have any skills or confidence in herself. However, Mrs. Jolson kept encouraging Hannah by saying, "I have faith that you can do this."

Hannah was not at all happy. She had never had to cook at home and felt very picked on. After realizing they were not going to let her off the hook, Hannah chose spaghetti with sauce, as it seemed pretty easy. Mrs. Jolson stood by and helped her learn how to work the stove and to learn where everything was. It reminded Mom that cooking is really pretty complicated. Her children had been cooking for so long that she had forgotten that it takes some thinking to get it all organized so that all of dinner is ready about the same time. Because she had had no previous training for this task, Hannah did not feel confident, so Mrs. Jolson helped as part of her training period.

When Hannah's turn came around the third week, she wanted Mrs. Jolson to "keep her company"—and help her. Mrs. Jolson declined, partly because she had a project she needed to finish, and partly because she had confidence (more than Hannah did) that she could do it on her own.

Hannah came to Mrs. Jolson to ask how to turn the oven on and for a preparation hint. She showed her how to turn on the oven (again) and answered her questions. At the very end, Mrs. Jolson joined her in the kitchen to help coordinate getting things on the table. After that, Mrs. Jolson stayed out of the kitchen while Hannah took her turn to cook.

For the next few weeks, choosing a menu was still hard. Because she was inexperienced, figuring out how to make a balanced meal was a challenge. (Permissive, pampering parents don't realize how much they contribute to the lack of confidence and skills in their children.) As Hannah ate dinner with the family every night, however, she soon learned about the many possibilities for main dishes and side dishes.

After seven weeks, Mrs. Jolson noticed that Hannah had learned how to choose a menu and make a balanced dinner *all* by herself! Hannah was obviously pleased with what she had done. She told Mrs. Jolson that she wanted to have her family share cooking like this when she got home. She shared that her mom does all the cooking, but she doesn't really like to cook so she puts things together from packages. Hannah said, "It would be nice if everybody helped and could cook for each other, and the food would be better." That made Mrs. Jolson feel good, too, because she knew that Hannah felt like she was part of the family and enjoyed knowing she could also give to the family.

Permissiveness and Television

The issue of television watching seems like much more than simple permissiveness. Parents may think they are doing their children a favor by letting them have their own TV in their room. After all, it solves the problem of fighting over the remote control and deciding who gets to watch what. But television can become addictive. Too many people channel surf because they can't find anything worth watching, yet they can't stand to turn off the TV. What happens to relationships and the quality of life when vegging out in front of the TV becomes a habit?

Lack of Connection

Parents aren't thinking about the long-range results of providing each child with his or her own television. A huge factor in families today is the lack of connection. Parents are often too busy trying to get everything done and forget to take time to connect with their children in meaningful ways. Too many parents say their first priority in life is their children, but their actions show otherwise. Allowing children to have their own TV only increases the disconnection. It may seem easier to have the children "out of your hair"—until you consider the long-range results.

Television and Sleep Patterns

In addition, many parents don't think about how TV affects their children's sleep. Consider the results of a 1999 study by the pediatric sleep disorders clinic at Hasbro Children's Hospital in Providence, Rhode Island (affiliated with Brown University). This study has shown that allowing children to watch television before bed (especially stimulating, disturbing, or violent programs) leads to problems with both bedtime and sleep patterns.

What does this have to do with permissiveness and pampering? Well, parental edicts to turn off the television lead to a great many arguments and power struggles. (How many parents have found themselves wrestling with a three-year-old for control of the remote?) Of the parents in the study, 76 percent reported that they allowed their children to watch TV as part of their bedtime routine; 15.6 percent said their kids fall asleep in front of the TV. The parents in the study believed television had nothing to do with their children's sleep problems. The study authors said that eliminating TV completely was not nec-

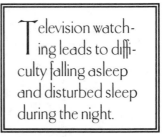

Television watching leads to difficulty falling asleep and disturbed sleep during the night.

essary, but they did recommend bedtime routines that did not include TV or videos but rather conversation and reading.

Other studies have shown that television is linked to depression, obesity, anxiety, and violent behavior in children. The American Academy of Pediatrics has recommended no television (yes, you read that correctly) for children under the age of two, saying it interferes with interpersonal relationships necessary for healthy development.

But there is another way. Just as giving up control does not mean that the only alternative is permissiveness, giving up permissiveness does not mean returning to excessive control. What children need are reasonable limits and structure.

Reasonable Limits and Structure

As we are discovering, one of the most loving things a parent can provide for a child is discipline, the sort of discipline that teaches skills and attitudes. An essential part of loving discipline is the ability to set (and follow through with) reasonable limits. Children themselves recognize that they need limits. In unguarded moments, teenagers will often comment on the failure of teachers and parents to provide the right sort of structure. Preschoolers respond well to discipline in the form of routines (bedtime, morning, after school, etc.). Therapists and child development experts often refer to misbehavior as "boundary testing," a child's way of conducting a scientific experiment to discover whether the adults in charge are doing their job.

> Limit setting is more effective when it is done with an attitude of maintaining dignity and respect for all concerned instead of an authoritarian, controlling attitude.

Recognizing and responding to limits are a part of life in a civilized society, a part that parents who love too much may struggle with. Permissive parents often fail to set limits at all. Controlling parents set far too many. What are "reasonable" limits? There are two things to consider:

1. Keep in mind the long-range purpose and goal of limits. Limits are necessary to improve the quality of life for both children and adults. However, limits are beneficial to children only when they are designed to teach important life skills, such as self-discipline, responsibility, cooperation, social interest, and problem-solving skills.
2. The attitude behind what you do is more important than what you do. Limit setting is more effective when it is done with an attitude of maintaining dignity and respect for all concerned instead of with an authoritarian, controlling attitude. The key to achieving this attitude is to get the child involved in the creation of limits whenever possible.

It is also important to consider developmental appropriateness. When children are younger than four years old, limit setting is the responsibility of adults. Adults draw the boundaries for children, such as eating and sleeping times, what they can and cannot touch, and where they can and cannot go. Enforcing limits at this age is most effective through regular routines, extremely limited choices ("Do you want to wear your blue pajamas or your yellow ones?"), distraction that is kind and firm, and learning how to hear and say no with dignity and respect.

As children get older, long-range life skills can be achieved when children are involved in setting limits.

Family meetings are great places to involve children in setting limits and to discuss with them which limits are useful and why. As with young children, routines are a great way to establish limits. Children are much more enthusiastic about and much more likely to honor and follow limits and routines they have helped establish. Routines can be written up on a chart (preferably by a child who is old enough) so the chart becomes the "boss." When children wander away from the routine, parents can avoid lectures and nagging simply by referring to the chart and asking questions such as "What is next on our chart?" or "What was our agreement? Let's check the chart."

> Imagine what the world would be like if all of the limits were reasonable, everyone respected them, and governments focused on solutions rather than punishment.

An important part of limit setting is follow-through. Grandmas around the world have had the right idea when they said, "Say what you mean and mean what you say!" We have just mentioned one method of follow-through—referring to a routine chart. Another effective way to follow through is to use *one* word to remind children of what needs to be done: "Toys. Jackets. Books. Bedtime. Respect." Kindly and firmly repeat the word until children realize that there isn't room for argument. (Remember, this is most effective if the children have helped create the rules and the routines.)

Sometimes parents need to "shut their mouths and act" by quietly, kindly, and firmly taking children by the hand and leading them away from what they shouldn't be doing or toward what they should be doing. Sometimes it is effective to decide what *you* will do instead of what you are going to try to make children do. Parents might decide they will only drive when children are not fighting or only cook after the kitchen has been cleaned. Deciding what *you* will do is most effective when you let your children know in advance what you are going to do under certain circumstances, and then follow through with what you have declared kindly and firmly—without further lectures.

Whenever a routine or limit isn't working, it helps to discuss the problem during a family meeting and engage children in problem solving. Children are amazingly good at brainstorming and solving problems when they are taught the skills and then allowed to participate. (Remember, it is always more effective to focus on *solutions* than on punishments or "consequences," an idea we will explore in greater detail later on.)

Part of providing structure for children includes teaching moral values and spirituality (see chapter 9). Obviously, the specifics of these values will vary from family to family, but a great deal of research has supported the idea that nurturing spirituality (a connection to something or someone greater than oneself—not, incidentally, the same thing as religiosity) and teaching morality are not only parts of healthy love, but also essential to healthy personhood. Setting reasonable limits, providing structure, and engaging children in the process of solving problems is one of the most loving things parents can do.

Imagine what the world would be like if all of the limits were reasonable, everyone respected them, and governments focused on solutions rather than punishment. It may never happen on a global scale, but it certainly can happen in your family when you give up both excessive control and permissiveness and use kind and firm parenting.

CHAPTER 5

Why Now?

The Reasons We Love Too Much

Just for the moment, let's accept that it's true: parents often do ineffective and ultimately damaging things in the name of love. Why does that happen? And why now? Have parents *always* loved too much or is this sort of love a modern innovation?

Conventional "Wisdom" and the Myths of Good Parenting

A huge shift in our thinking as a society about children has occurred. In the "good old days," people often said that children should be "seen but not heard." Children were viewed as "assets" to help on the farm or potential apprentices to continue their father's work; their happiness was not of paramount importance. (Of course, most adults were more concerned about survival than happiness themselves.) In fact, until fairly recently, children were seen as small containers of "original sin," more wicked than delightful and in dire need of "the rod" to be saved. The notion of helping a child build self-esteem had not been invented.

Paradoxically, although life was less luxurious, many children learned valuable skills and developed perceptions of capability in the process of working alongside their parents—skills and perceptions that formed the foundation of true self-esteem. Many of those who didn't have the opportunity to work alongside their parents learned "street smarts" because they were not overly pampered or controlled. These days we worry about the self-esteem of children while creating an environment where they don't learn the skills and perceptions that would help them develop it.

This shift in thinking, which often dictates that children's happiness should come before the sanity and dignity of anyone else, has created some confusing and paradoxical *conventional wisdom* about good parenting. Much of this "wisdom" is erroneous and encompasses myths that must be examined.

Should Children Be the Center of the Universe?

Many parents have come to believe that children should be the center of the universe—that they must always come first, that they should always be happy (in fact, we confuse true self-esteem with the notion that children should always "feel good" about themselves and about life), and that every moment of a parent's life that isn't devoted to work and duty should be given to the children.

Parents have been inundated with parenting information and advice. (We confess we've contributed to the deluge—although we believe our approach is both useful and effective.) What has caused the shift toward such extremes as "attachment parenting" and the family bed? What happened to cause parents to worry that their children might suffer traumatic damage if they didn't receive the candy they demanded in the grocery store? When did parents decide they should get up at 2:00 A.M. to stand in line in the dark waiting for the department store to open so they could buy their child a Cabbage Patch doll, a Tickle Me Elmo, or the latest toy craze?

The answers are complicated, and there isn't just one. Some blame it on affluence, working women, child advocates, parenting experts, the loss of the extended family, child labor laws, or television. The reasons aren't as important as the effects. And as we have already seen, the effects of permissiveness and pampering are not healthy for children, parents, or society. Children who are raised permissively are likely to adopt the belief that "The world owes me a living" or "Love means getting others to take care of me" or "I should always have what I want—right now!"

Parents sometimes decide to raise their children just as they were raised. "It worked fine for me," they say with a bemused expression, "but it isn't working at all with my kids." Or they insist that they've raised their children in ways that avoid the mistakes their own parents made. "I swore I'd never do what my parents did," they say, "but my children still act like brats. Why?"

Why, indeed. Parents often repeat their own parents' mistakes, or they go to the opposite extreme; neither is likely to be effective. The fact is that the world in which we and our children live now bears very little resemblance to the one in which most of us grew up. Oh, some things haven't changed: We're born, we grow up, we may search for a partner, we may choose to have children, we work and have dreams, we struggle, we hope to succeed. But our society, our technology, our culture, the pressures we experience, and our own expectations conspire to make it surprisingly difficult to have fulfilling marriages and children who thrive as adults. There are a number of reasons why this is so:

- Changes in our society, particularly since World War II
- The entrance of women into the full-time workforce and the resulting issues of child care and stress (and, as we will see, guilt—lots and lots of guilt)
- Changes in our families, including the divorce rate, the increasing number of single-parent families and stepfamilies, and the tendency of American families to be separated from extended family members
- Changes in our culture, which now stresses mass media, technology, and individual activities rather than involvement in a larger community
- The gradual shift toward putting children at the center of the family universe and indulging their whims and desires, often at the expense of adults

- Parents' "loving ignorance"—their failure to recognize these changes and adapt their parenting approach accordingly, and their inability to learn and practice long-range parenting skills

America Since World War II

Most historians and sociologists believe that World War II forever changed life in this country. Before the 1940s, most Americans lived off the land or in small communities. Most wives and mothers remained in the home raising children while the men went off to work each day. The war changed everything. Men were needed to do the fighting, but someone had to work in the factories, keep the communities running, and produce the goods needed to fight a major war. "Rosie the Riveter" was born—and when the war ended, she wasn't always willing to go back to the kitchen.

Many families decided they liked this more modern life. Gradually, the population shifted from the country to the city, where the best jobs were usually found. Children, parents, and grandparents were less likely to live in the same home; increasingly, they didn't even live in the same city or state, and young parents lost a valuable source of support and advice. New industries arose; new products were readily available, and more families had the money to buy them. Many adults can remember their family's first radio, first car, first television, first *color* television. It became possible to have lots of "things"; eventually, it became *important* to have lots of things. And as time passed, many couples decided that one working adult just wasn't enough.

The Birth of the Working Mom

There are almost as many reasons why women work for a living as there are women who work. Regardless of what you believe about working mothers, the fact is that there are legions of them these days. In 1950, 12 percent of mothers with children younger than six worked outside the home; today, 50 percent of mothers with children younger than three and an astonishing 75 percent of mothers with school-age children work. When women work, someone else has to watch the kids. The swelling number of women in the workforce has created an entirely new industry (and a new variable in children's lives): child care.

The jury is still out on the effect of working mothers and child care on children, particularly on young children. But there is no question that whatever the benefits may be, working women have difficult choices to make about how they spend the time they're not at work, how to manage the stress created by having two working parents, and where children fit in their lives.

Rosalie, 36, has a high-powered job with an advertising firm in New York. Her husband, Cliff, is an attorney with a prestigious law firm in Chicago. Rosalie commutes from the family's home in a Chicago suburb to her job (and an apartment) in New York. She has a

"European-trained" nanny who lives in to take care of her two children, who are four and seven years old. Cliff spends as much time as he can with the children, but he often has to work late.

Rosalie remembers that her own mother was always home when Rosalie came in from school; she feels rather guilty about missing so much of her children's lives and complains about the time she spends flying back and forth. But Rosalie believes that her job makes it possible for the family—and the children—to have the lifestyle she's always dreamed of. The children have everything, she says proudly, and she and Cliff are very careful about hiring only the best nannies. Yes, she's usually too tired when she's at home to go to soccer games or have tea parties, but she bristles when anyone suggests her choices may be harming her children. "They know I love them," she says firmly. "I always bring them a present from New York. And we'll have more time together later on."

Are Rosalie's choices harming her children? She undoubtedly loves them, but is supplying them with a "lifestyle" and the best child care truly *healthy* love? It's safe to say that most working mothers, even those with far less demanding jobs than Rosalie's, wonder from time to time whether they have enough energy to go around, whether they can be a "good" parent and partner and a healthy individual. (Incidentally, stay-at-home parents often feel guilty because they *don't* work. Are they depriving their children of advantages and opportunities?) Many parents—mothers and fathers alike—

resort to control or permissiveness because stress, guilt, and limited time make it seem like the only way.

The atmosphere is very different in Cecelia's family. Cecelia is a single mom[1] who works full time in a dental office to provide for herself and her three children, ages three, six, and eight. Cecelia found and hired another single mom, Sharon, who takes care of Cecelia's children during the workday.

Cecelia means it when she says her children come first in her life. She does not use tiredness as an excuse for not spending time with them. Instead, she has involved her children in helping her to create routines. They all work together and then have more time to play together.

True, they don't have a lot of "things." Cecelia has started engaging her six- and eight-year-old children in discussions about the dangers of materialism. During family meetings they discuss together what their priorities are and how to budget their money to accomplish their goals. They have decided together that they will eat fast food only twice a month so they can save money toward a camping vacation at the beach.

Cecelia lets her children know how much she needs them, but does not put excessive pressure on them. The children have many opportunities to experience how capable they are. They plans meals together at their weekly family meetings, and each child is "in charge" of the cooking two nights a week—with lots of help from Mom.

---

1. We do not believe single-parent families are "broken" families; they are simply another kind of family. See *Positive Discipline for Single Parents*, by Jane Nelsen, Cheryl Erwin, and Carol Delzer (Prima, 1999).

Too often, working parents or single parents are blamed for every ill in the world. We seem to ignore the fact that there are still more good people in our society than "bad," and that many of them are being or were raised in single-parent families or in families in which both parents worked.

The factor that most people fail to consider when speculating on the causes of the many problems in our society is this: do these parents love too much in unhealthy ways? We know of no research that proves it, but we hypothesize that problems relate more to the type of parenting (specifically, the degree of long-range thinking that takes place) than to factors such as single parenthood or economic prosperity.

Divorce, American-Style

Working moms aren't the only change in our society. The very nature of families has been transformed in the past few decades. Like it or not, the 1960s ushered in the sexual revolution. Moral values relaxed; people married later in life; divorce became easier, more common, and less shameful; and the traditional nuclear family was gradually replaced by a host of variations: single-parent families, stepfamilies, gay and lesbian parents, grandparents raising their grandchildren. In fact, statistics tell us that as of 2000, the most common form of family in this country is the stepfamily, and the failure rate for second or third marriages is currently even higher (as high as 70 percent in some studies) than that for first marriages.

A University of Chicago study made it clear how sweeping these changes have been. Among the findings:

1. In 1998, 56 percent of adults were married, compared with nearly 75 percent in 1972.
2. Fifty-one percent of children lived in a household with both of their parents, versus 73 percent in 1972. Eighteen percent of all children live with single parents.
3. Values have changed as well. In 1972 and now, parents listed "thinking for themselves" as their most valued trait in their children. But in 1972, obedience was second, and hard work was third. Today obedience has dropped in popularity; parents say they want their children to be "self-disciplined" and believe children should have more autonomy. They also want children to have fun, but in organized ways that suit parents' busy schedules. Open-ended play requiring adult supervision is now less acceptable than organized "drop-off" activities, such as gymnastics and soccer.

All of these changes have staggering implications for children. We believe that *any* family can be a healthy, nurturing place for children to grow and learn, but it certainly does take a bit more thought and planning these days. Many parents share custody and find it tempting to compensate children for divorces, lack of time, and absent parents by giving them things and privileges. Loving children too much becomes even more damaging when there are two or more parents doing it! Many parents face a sort of "double whammy"; they are single, divorced, or remarried *and* they work; the temptation to relax limits and compensate with things or to attempt to seize control of their children's behavior can be overwhelming. After all, children of divorced or single parents are more likely to be delinquents—aren't they? (In a word, no.)

The Cultural Revolution

Few families—even those with minimum income—go without television. Television can be a marvelous tool for communication and education, but it inadvertently created an entirely new industry: advertising. Each year, billions of dollars are spent in an effort to sell Americans name-brand clothing, toys, and entire lifestyles, and many of those dollars are directed at children. Until quite recently, a great deal of children's television programming was thinly disguised advertising for toys and other products. Children who have been "sold" on the idea that they must have the latest cool toy or outfit can become adept at wheedling and manipulating parents—who often feel guilty already and are unduly tempted to give in.

Televisions are everywhere; it is not uncommon for children to have TVs, VCRs, and video games in their rooms. In many, many families, "family time" consists of each member alone in a room with his or her own television. Gone are the days when the entire family would gather around the set to watch a favorite program or a news event; these days, television often serves to isolate us from each other, not to draw us together. Are parents considering the long-range results when they allow their children to have so many "things" in their own rooms? Too often, children's rooms are crammed with evidence that their parents love them too much—without thought for the consequences.

The Internet also has complicated life for families. Most parents want their children to be computer-literate; it is, after all, becoming a necessary skill for success in almost every field. But the Internet, too, is awash in advertising. Much of the material available is inappropriate for children, and too many parents lack the skill and vigilance to ensure that their children are using computers wisely. Family members have their own computers, too—one more reason not to spend time talking and listening to each other. Are parents considering the long-range results (and very real risks) when they allow their children to spend time on the Internet alone in their rooms? Sexual predators prowl the Internet; all sorts of material of a seductive and illicit nature is available, and many experts now recognize that computers can become a powerful addiction. However, many pre-teens and teens are not spending time looking at sexual Web sites. Many like to spend hours and hours in chat rooms engaged in what may seem to be meaningless chit-chat, similar to the way they spend hours on the phone or in the mall talking with friends.

> Learning to manage our ever-increasing technology is an important part of loving children in healthy ways.

Sad as it may seem, many young people today are far more familiar with their favorite musical artists, celebrities, and television characters than they are with members of their own families. It may be convenient to use the television or computer as a baby-sitter while you prepare dinner or clean the house, but it doesn't encourage the development of healthy skills, beliefs, and relationships with your children. Learning to manage our ever-increasing technology is an important part of loving children in healthy ways.

The "Experts" Disagree, and Parents Are Confused

Parenting in the modern world has become remarkably complicated. Few if any parents make it through their children's first three years of life without buying or being given one parenting manual, and most wind up with a shelf full. Parenting advice isn't new; there were parenting experts in the 1800s (all men, of course; women weren't thought to be able to understand the complexities of child rearing). One Dr. Luther Holt of Columbia University, for example, warned parents of the "vicious practice" of using a comfortable cradle, picking up a child when it cried, or holding it too often.

Dr. Spock is probably the best known of the modern generation of parenting experts, but he has been followed by a stampede of others, often with wildly conflicting views. William Sears, for instance, advocates sleeping with your children in a "family bed" and being in constant physical contact with them, almost never putting them down; John Rosemond encourages parents to just tell kids, "Because I said so!" The Bible is used to advocate spanking; other experts stake out territory somewhere in between. Judith Rich Harris in "The Nurture Assumption" tells parents that what they do with and to their children doesn't affect their adult behavior and personality at all—only their genes and peers do. And most parents are terribly confused.

One mom who wound up with her children sleeping in her bed described herself as "sleepwalking along the path of least resistance." In other words, she started sleeping with her children because it was easy and keeps sleeping with them because it seems too difficult to stop. (After all, they would undoubtedly cry.) Because she doesn't want her children to experience the pain of breaking this habit (and because she is usually weary herself), she has discovered "experts" who helped her justify what she is doing.

Many parents read lots of books—and feel more confused and overwhelmed than if they'd remained uneducated. They try one technique after another, none of which seems to work the way they hope it will; their frustration and discouragement with "modern parenting" sometimes leads them to give up and give in (permissiveness) or attempt to take over (control).

We believe that following a single parenting technique (e.g., time-out, "1, 2, 3 Magic," or setting "consequences") often leads parents onto dangerous ground. These methods often provide temporary results with no consideration for what children are thinking, feeling, and deciding about themselves and their future behavior. Too many parenting methods do not consider long-range results. They are more concerned with stopping behavior "now" than with the skills their children are learning. Education and knowledge are vital; we believe that parents must understand their children's development, temperaments, limitations, and what is effective in the long run.

Trusting Your Own Heart and Wisdom

Education is not enough in and of itself; parents must be able to choose from the many parenting tools and techniques available (including the ones we teach) those that "fit" for them. Parents must learn to trust their own wisdom and common sense, to be the "experts" for their own children—something that is easier to do when you understand child development, have learned to get into your child's world, and have given some thought to the importance of long-range parenting. Without this kind of knowledge, "what fits for you" may be based solely on emotional reactions instead of wisdom.

Loving Too Much for the Neighbors

Some parents are more concerned about what the neighbors think than what they think themselves (or what really works for their children). In the following story, you will see how Mindy recognized this fact when she visited the "magic store."

In group therapy there is a technique called the "magic store." The idea is to go to the magic store and choose anything you want—and then pay the price. An effective "store clerk" (therapist) has clever ways of helping "customers" at the magic store gain profound insights by suggesting the "price" one has to pay for the person, thing, or circumstance that is desired.

Mindy volunteered to play magic store at her counseling group. When the clerk asked, "What do you want more than anything else in the world?" Mindy replied, "To be a good mother."

The clerk then asked a profound question: "For whom? For the neighbors, for your in-laws, or for your children?" Mindy was stunned when she realized she had been more concerned about what others thought of her parenting methods than what her children thought. She worried more about what others thought she *should* do than about searching for what made sense to her and what helped create the sort of adults she wanted her children to become.

> Parents must learn to trust their own wisdom and common sense, to be the "experts" for their own children.

This was the beginning of a transformation for Mindy as she began questioning the "conventional wisdom" of others. She began an intensive education program in parenting. She read books and attended parenting classes.

Perhaps most important, she began to filter everything she learned through her own inner wisdom, and slowly she became more interested in the long-range benefits to her children than what the neighbors might think. She began considering the decisions her children were making about future behavior and the sort of people they would become. Not surprisingly, she discovered that both her children's behavior and her relationship with them improved considerably.

Social Pressure

It takes a great deal of courage to overcome social pressure and to follow your heart and inner wisdom instead of doing what you think others expect or will approve of. (Is any mother totally immune to the mother-in-law who comments sourly, "*My* children never whined like yours do.") Parents are, understandably enough, sensitive to the opinions of those around them: teachers and school administrators, neighbors, friends and leaders at church, other parents at Little League games. Deciding what makes sense for your own child, your own family, takes courage and thoughtfulness.

For example, one summer the Johnsons went backpacking with several friends. Their ten-year-old son Jason was a very good sport and carried his pack the long six miles into the canyon. When they were getting ready for the steep trek back out, Jason complained about how uncomfortable his pack was. His dad jokingly remarked, "You can take it. You're the son of a Marine."

Jason was in too much pain to think this was very funny, but he started the climb anyway. He hadn't gone very far ahead of the rest of the group when they heard his pack come crashing down the hill toward them. Mom was alarmed, thinking he had fallen and hurt himself. She rushed to his side and saw with relief that he was alive and unharmed. She asked with concern, "Are you okay? What happened?"

Jason angrily cried, "Nothing! It just hurts!"

He turned around and continued climbing without his pack. The rest of the group watched with interest. One adult offered to carry the pack for him. Jason's mom was feeling very embarrassed and wondered how she should react to her son's behavior. Would her friends think she was a bad parent?

After a moment (and a deep breath), she overcame her ego and remembered that the most important thing was to solve the problem in a way that would help Jason feel encouraged and responsible. She asked the rest of the party to please hike on ahead so that they could handle the problem in private. She then realized how important it was to *get into Jason's world* and understand what was going on for him before they could focus on solutions.

Mom said to Jason, "I'll bet you feel really angry that we wouldn't pay serious attention when you tried to tell us your pack hurt before we even started."

Jason said, "Yeah, and I'm not carrying it!"

Mom replied, "I don't blame you; I'd feel exactly the same way if I were you."

Jason's dad was standing nearby listening and soon caught the spirit of what was happening. He told Jason he was sorry for his thoughtless remark and asked for another chance to solve the problem.

Jason visibly released his anger. He was now ready to cooperate. He and his dad figured out a way to stuff his coat over the sore part to cushion the pack. Jason carried his pack the rest of the way with only a few minor complaints.

Of course, the Johnsons could not really know what their friends expected, but if they had tried to guess, they might have given Jason a stern lecture about his irresponsible behavior and punished him so their friends would know they weren't letting Jason get away with anything. In other words, they would be more interested in *looking* good than in *being* good. They would be more interested in short-term effects of pleasing the neighbors than the long-term results of teaching their son communication and problem-solving skills. Instead of following their own common sense, they would be lost in a mire of confusion.

Who's Most Important? The Children!

We will stress over and over that long-range parenting considers what is best for children in the long term, rather that what feels best or is most expedient in the moment. It means that putting children first and worrying about their short-term happiness usually is not the most healthy sort of loving.

As parents have become more stressed, guilty, and overwhelmed, children (and their constant happiness) have become more and more important. As we have seen, children rule the roost in most families; giving them what they want and attempting to "nurture their self-esteem" keep parents running twenty-four hours a day.

> Long-range parenting considers what is best for children in the long term, rather than what feels best or is most expedient in the moment.

Children who are indulged, pampered, and showered with undivided attention miss the opportunity to learn the skills and attitudes that will help them become healthy adults. What are parents thinking when they make children's happiness their top priority (as long as it's fairly convenient, that is)? They are thinking short-term rather than long-range. They are giving in to expediency, momentary good feelings, and emotions—and one of the most powerful is guilt.

Guilt

One of the first steps toward overcoming the trap of loving too much is to understand the role guilt plays in your parenting style. Guilt is a huge factor; in fact, it affects so many parents so deeply that it deserves an entire chapter—the next one. (We should note that we are experts on the effects of guilt, having experienced so much of it ourselves.) It is possible to avoid "loving too much." It is our goal as authors to help you avoid unhealthy loving and to help you understand the best way to do this—for yourself and for your children. Giving up guilt may be the first step.

CHAPTER 6

Guilt

The Root of Loving Too Much

How often is guilt the primary motivator for the extremes of loving too much? Too often—in fact, guilt is the common denominator of many poor parenting choices. Parents feel guilty if they work, if they are single, if they are widowed, if they are poor, if they are busy, if they aren't spending enough time with their children. In today's complicated world, there are literally hundreds of reasons for parents to feel guilty.

There are two problems with guilt as a motivator. First, what good does it do to feel guilty about something you can't (or won't) change? Second, what good does it do to feel guilty about something if you *can* change it?

When Guilt Is Used
as an Excuse for Avoiding Change

Guilt is often our disguise for doing "bad" while feeling "good." In other words, parents sometimes justify their actions by saying, "At least I feel guilty. I would be a really bad person if I did this and didn't feel guilty." It is far more productive to stop feeling guilty and change your behavior *or* to stop feeling guilty and do what you are doing with confidence and satisfaction. Let's examine some of the areas where parents feel guilty and how to either change or accept the circumstances.

Single-Parent Guilt

Most people these days can tell you that the divorce rate in this country has hovered for years at about 50 percent: half of all marriages end in divorce. (The number is even higher for second and third marriages.) This fact leads to another: there are many single parents in the world and many children who are growing up in single-parent homes. Many single parents harbor deep fears that their children will be damaged forever because they are not being raised by two parents. The truth is that many wonderful, successful people have been raised by single parents. When

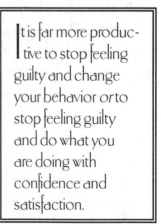

It is far more productive to stop feeling guilty and change your behavior *or* to stop feeling guilty and do what you are doing with confidence and satisfaction.

single parents feel guilty, they often resort to the extremes that come from loving too much, which may take several forms.

1. Trying to "make it up" to their poor, deprived children. Single parents often treat their children (and themselves) as victims who need sympathy. These parents may knock themselves out trying to be both a mother and a father to their children. Attitudes are contagious; children quickly pick up the victim mentality and feel sorry for themselves. Or children may assume that they are at a disadvantage (or entitled to special treatment) because they have a single parent. Such decisions do not lead to positive long-term results, for parents or for children.

2. Trying to provide material goodies even when they can't afford it. It is sad—and ultimately not helpful to children—when single parents are unable to say, "We can't afford that," with confidence and dignity. The inability to provide material goods can be a blessing in disguise (and an opportunity to teach valuable life skills) when approached with a positive attitude.

3. Trying to provide too much emotional support when they are emotionally drained themselves. Most single parents can tell you about the times they have sat and listened while a child weeps for his lost family or a missing parent. They will tell you it is a helpless, often hopeless feeling. It is tempting to want to "fix" a child's feeling, to talk him out of his grief or anger, to protect him from suffering pain. Sometimes parents erupt into anger themselves, either at the child or at the partner who is no longer there. Not only can parents not rescue their children from their feelings, but it is also rarely helpful even to try. Because single parents are often grieving, overwhelmed, or exhausted themselves, their ability to handle their child's strong emotions may be limited.

All of us must learn to deal with grief, disappointment, and anger, as we will see throughout this book. Parents who demonstrate their love for their children in ineffective ways may try to protect their children from these experiences—and their children miss the opportunity to learn that they are capable of dealing with (and learning from) life's traumas.

4. Resorting to excessive control in the name of "saving" children from their inevitable fate. Most single parents have heard somewhere that children growing up in single-parent homes are more likely to fall victim to drugs, premature sexual activity, academic difficulties, crime, and delinquency. Many overreact by trying to provide "discipline" in the form of strict rules, constant supervision, and punishments. As we have already learned, parents try to control their children's behavior for a variety of excellent reasons—but excessive control inevitably fails to produce the desired results in children. Being a single parent is a tough job, but kind and firm parenting works as well for single parents as it does for married ones.

Stepfamily Guilt

There is a common corollary to single-parent guilt— stepfamily guilt. Most single parents eventually remarry, and stepfamilies can be very complicated places in which to live. Children struggle with divided loyalties and often must cope with regular transitions between homes with different rules and expectations. Parents see their children's struggle to adjust, and they end up feeling guilty, guilty, guilty. After all, what if children don't like their new stepparent? What if they miss their own parent or must share a parent with stepsiblings? What if, as so often happens, a father lives with his new wife and her children while his own birth children, with whom he "should" be spending his time, live somewhere else? Stepfamilies present dozens of seemingly good reasons to feel guilty and to cope by going to extremes.

Regardless of their marital situation, parents must face their own feelings and invest the time it takes to become healthy themselves; they can also have faith in a child's ability to survive his feelings. Single, step-, and married parents can practice reflective listening ("I know how much you're missing your dad right now"), offer a hug, and, when appropriate, involve the child in brainstorming for possible solutions. Empathy and compassion, coupled with kind and firm parenting, are not only "enough," they are also all that a wise parent can truly offer. (For additional suggestions on living as part of a stepfamily or in a single-parent home, see *Positive Discipline for Single Parents*, rev. 2nd ed., Prima, 2000, and *Positive Discipline for Your Stepfamily*, rev. 2nd ed., Prima, 2000.)

Working-Parent Guilt

Some parents work because they have to. Others work because they want to. In either case, many parents are afraid their children will suffer if there is not at least one parent who stays home. Media "experts," such as Dr. Laura, have exacerbated the problem by asserting that "good" parents always stay at home with their children ("Hi! I'm my kid's

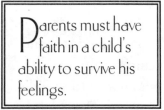

Parents must have faith in a child's ability to survive his feelings.

mom!"). Parents who believe their children will suffer when they work spend a lot of time feeling guilty. Children sense the guilt and learn to use it to their advantage.

"Read Me Another Story": The Saga of Guilt-Anger-Remorse-Guilt-Anger-Remorse-Guilt

"Read me another story," whined four-year-old Angela. Chris was tired—she had a report to prepare for a presentation the next day—and now she was getting angry. She had already given in to her daughter's pleas for three stories, and she didn't want to read another. But she felt undeniably guilty for leaving Angela at the day care center while she worked all day. After all, her own mother had been home every afternoon when she returned from school, and Chris had a nagging feeling that she needed to make it up to Angela, even though she felt frustrated and irritable because she also needed some time to herself. So she sighed, gave in, and grumpily read Angela a fourth story.

When Angela whined for one more, Chris found herself quite suddenly at the end of her rope. She scolded, "Angela, you are never satisfied. I'm *never* going to read you another story because you just want more, more, more. You can just do without until you learn to appreciate what you get!"

Angela burst into sobs. Chris ran to the bathroom, locked the door, and burst into sobs herself. Then she remorsefully began scolding herself. "She's only a child who wants to spend some time with me. If I'm going to leave her alone all day, the least I can do is read her as many stories as she wants." Then the guilt started again. "It isn't her fault that I'm tired. I don't want my little girl to suffer because she has a working mom. How will I ever manage?"

What is truth and what is fiction regarding this scene? It is true that Angela needs time with her mom. It is fiction that she needs to hear four stories. When Chris allows Angela to push her "guilt button," she is teaching Angela the skill of manipulation.

When Chris learns to allot a reasonable amount of time for her bedtime routine with Angela, she can avoid the anger stage. After one or two stories (in whatever time Chris can give with enjoyment—and without resentment), she can say kindly and firmly, "Story time is over. Time for my hug and kiss."

Angela will know whether her mom means what she says, just as she will know whether her mom's guilt button is still available for pushing. However, while Chris is learning to give up her guilt button, it will only be natural for Angela to up the ante in an attempt to keep the old game going. She may scream, "I want another story!"

Again, kindly and firmly, Chris can say, "Do you want to go to sleep without a hug and kiss or with a hug and kiss?" This may be enough to distract Angela from the power struggle by giving her an opportunity to use her power to make a choice. If Angela keeps whining or screaming, however, Chris can say, "I'll just sit here for five minutes to see if that is enough time for you to get ready for a hug and kiss." (After all, Chris helped Angela perfect her manipulation skills. It may take patience for her to learn mutual respect.) If Angela continues the manipulation pattern, Chris can say, "I can see you're not ready for a hug and kiss now. We'll try again tomorrow night," and then leave. (Yes, Angela will cry. And crying is rarely if ever fatal.)

There are several ways to eliminate the working-parent guilt-anger-remorse cycle.

1. Give up your guilt buttons. Children can thrive with working parents. When you have confidence in this fact, your guilt buttons will disappear. By the way, children always know when you have guilt buttons that can be pushed, and they know when you don't. Guilt buttons send out a certain kind of energy that speaks louder than words. It won't help to listen to Dr. Laura repeat every day, "I am my kid's mom," and imply that parents should never work. You can chant your own daily mantra with pride, "I am my kid's *working* mom," and have confidence that you and your kids can be just fine—if you can give up your guilt, consider long-range results, and engage in kind and firm parenting.

It may help you relax to know that as a rule, children do not resent their parents for working. Ellen Galinsky, author of *Ask the Children* (William Morrow, 1999), interviewed more than a thousand children in grades 3 through 12. These children were asked to "grade" their parents on twelve areas strongly linked to healthy development. Having a mother who worked was never once predictive of how children assessed their mother's parenting skills.

> When you have confidence in the fact that children can thrive with working parents, your guilt buttons will disappear.

In fact, many children expressed pride in their parents' willingness to work hard and reported that they felt more secure when the family was financially stable. They felt less respect for fathers who did not work. What kids objected to was not too little time with parents but time with parents that felt rushed or begrudged or was not rich in real connection. About 44 percent of these children said their time with Mom felt rushed; 37 percent felt their time with Dad was too hurried. In addition, parents sometimes don't get the message: only 33 percent of the parents thought their time with their children was rushed.

Working in and of itself does not damage children. As with so many other aspects of parenting, attitude is everything. Considering the long-range results of your current choices (and what your children are deciding as a result) may help you improve your effectiveness and give up your working-parent guilt.

2. Avoid pampering in the name of guilt or for any other reason. When parents feel guilty about working, they often try to assuage their guilt through pampering. As we have seen, pampering is not healthy for children. First, children learn far more from our actions than they do from our words: they can sense what you are doing and why (even if subconsciously), and they "know" that you think they are being deprived. If you believe this, why shouldn't they? Second, pampering invites children to form unhealthy beliefs such as "I feel loved only if I'm pampered" or "I'm entitled to special service." Third, they learn unhealthy manipulation skills instead of respectful life skills. With kind and firm parenting, your children can develop respectful life skills such as self-discipline, responsibility, cooperation, and problem solving.

3. Decide what you are willing to do, and state it specifically. Chris could tell Angela, "I will read two stories," and *mean* it. Again, confidence, kindness, and firmness are the keys. Deciding what you are willing to do is a demonstration of self-respect. The willingness to spend reasonable time and perform reasonable tasks for and with your children demonstrates respect for them. However, if you state your intentions in a threatening way instead of a respectful way, the effectiveness is diminished.

4. Avoid lectures and scoldings. When you don't feel guilty, there is no need to make your child feel guilty. Lectures and scoldings are usually designed to manipulate through guilt. Even if they work, the price in terms of lowered self-confidence in your children is a price that is too high to pay. Limit discipline words to ten or fewer. One word is often best: "Homework." "Dishes." "Bath." You can have faith that your children know what you mean, especially if you have discussed routines and procedures respectfully together, in advance, as described below. When your child pleads for another story, you might smile and say, "Bedtime," before leaving the room.

5. When you say it, mean it; and when you mean it, follow through with dignity and respect. Follow-through is often more effective when you avoid using words at all—as you know if you've ever found yourself in a heated debate with someone who only comes up to your kneecaps. Besides, have you noticed how often children (especially teenagers) use your words to defeat you?

Act instead. Let your kind and firm actions speak loud and clear. If you say you will read two stories, stick to your decision. At the end of the stories, give a hug and a kiss, and leave the room with confidence.

6. Plan ahead. Another way to avoid the "tell me another story" debate is to talk about it in advance. Engage your child in planning for the future. When you decide to make a change, it is respectful to let your child know and to work on a plan together.

Chris decided to try this approach with Angela. While driving home from day care one evening, Chris shared her feelings with Angela. "Sweetie, I love you so much. I want our time together to be happy time. I'll bet that you and I can figure out a plan to make bedtime a happy time. Okay?"

Angela caught the spirit of her mother's new attitude and said, "Okay."

Chris continued, "I'm willing to read two stories. I know it upsets you when I yell at you, and it upsets me when you whine for another story. What could we do instead after I read the stories?"

Angela said, "I know. You could give me a hug and kiss?" This was already part of their routine, but it seemed very different to Angela when it was her idea.

Chris said, "I like that idea. And why don't we figure out a signal that we can give each other to help us stop if we start getting upset? How about tugging on our ears or a wink, or do you have another idea?"

> When you decide to make a change, it is respectful to let your child know and to work on a plan together.

Angela said, "We could tap our knees."

Chris said, "Great. Let's try that."

That night their plan worked like a charm—because it was a plan that they had worked on together. This is why routines can be so effective. When parents and children plan routines together (bedtime routines, morning routines, mealtime routines), the routine becomes the boss. Parents can ask their children, "What is next in our bedtime routine?" Children feel empowered because they can check it out instead of being ordered by their parents and because they helped plan the routine in the first place.

7. Allow time for your child to adjust to your new behavior. Remember, you helped create the patterns that are now established. Change may take time. It may take a while for your child to believe your guilt button will not come back, that you mean what you say, and that you will behave respectfully, kindly, and firmly.

We repeat: *children can thrive with working parents.* Your attitude is the key. If you feel guilty and believe your children may suffer, they are likely to adopt your attitude—and to develop manipulation skills. If you feel confidence in your abilities and the abilities of your children to create a happy, successful home, they are more likely to adopt that attitude and to develop cooperation skills.

Child Care Guilt

Closely related to working-parent guilt is child care guilt; some parents even suffer from both at the same time. Selena, a single parent, and Rosie became friends when they both started working for a large corporation in their hometown. Both had found excellent child care for their three-year-old children. Selena lived next door to a widowed grandmother who was delighted to have the opportunity to take care of Selena's child. Rosie found a licensed preschool with an excellent reputation.

At the end of the day, both children would cling to their child care providers. They did not want to leave them. This caused Selena to feel agony. Rosie, however, felt relieved and happy.

Selena was jealous. She was afraid her child would love someone else more than her. Rosie was thrilled that her child was so loved and contented in her day care situation that she didn't want to leave. She was able to give up her guilt about working and having her child in child care when she knew her daughter was receiving so much love.

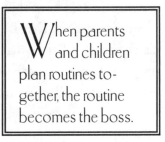

When parents and children plan routines together, the routine becomes the boss.

It helped Selena to talk to Rosie about her feelings. She realized that it didn't really make sense to feel bad about the fact that her child was happy and felt so loved by her neighbor. Selena let go of her jealousy and focused on her gratitude for finding such excellent child care.

The debate.   The debate goes on and on as to whether children do better when at least one parent stays home or whether they do just fine—if not better—in a quality day care situation. The results of several recent studies have suggested that children can thrive in quality day care. These studies found that "family factors" (primarily maternal sensitivity and responsiveness) appeared to be more powerful predictors than child care of children's eventual outcome—except, of course, for poor-quality child care (NICHD Early Child Care Research Network, "Characteristics of Infant Child Care: Factors

Contributing to Positive Caregiving," *Early Childhood Research Quarterly* 11 [1996]: 267–306). The results of the studies caused an uproar among the "moms should stay home" advocates.

The stay-at-home advocates claim that all the problems of youth today, such as drugs, vandalism, and teenage pregnancy, can be laid at the doorstep of working mothers. (Those that aren't being laid at the doorstep of single parents, that is.) We are not sure that these critics consider all the variables. Could it be that many of the problems have other causes, such as too much television, materialism, pampered children, or excessive control—the extremes we have been exploring? These problems exist in families where mothers stay home, as well as in families where mothers work, in both single-parent and two-parent homes.

We admit that we don't know which is best for your children or for you, to work or to stay home with them. We do believe, however, that whether you and your children succeed in either situation depends on your attitude, particular circumstances, and parenting skills.

Assets and liabilities for either situation. Let's be realistic. Neither working parents nor stay-at-home parents experience total joy and bliss all the time. Children, regardless of their situation, do not turn out "all good" or "all bad." There are assets and liabilities that go along with any decision and any situation. In all cases, helping children thrive can be a continuing challenge and a continuing joy. The best solution is to follow your heart, absorb all the knowledge you can, and then do your best and see all situations (including mistakes made by you and your children) as opportunities for learning.

Of course, some parents don't have the option of staying home. As we have said before, guilt is absolutely useless in a situation that can't be changed. What works is to make the best of whatever situation you have and discover ways to make it beneficial to all concerned—this plan is possible if you use understanding and creativity. The following story, also used in *Positive Discipline for Single Parents* (Prima, 2000), provides an excellent example of how a working single mom learned to stop loving too much, gave up her guilt, and found ways to work with her children that are empowering instead of discouraging to all of them.

Sandy is a single parent who runs a day care program in her home. She has two children of her own, four-year-old Kyle and six-year-old Joey. Sandy told her parenting group that she needed help. Near tears, she reported that Joey was driving her crazy while she tried to manage the day care program. "He taunts the younger children, hits them, takes their toys, and uses nasty language. He fights with the older boys over the use of the equipment. Joey's not having this trouble at school or at his friends' homes. He misbehaves only with me. He's so bad that I want to stop having the children come right now and give him the attention he needs. I think the day care is too hard for him to handle because I'm a single mom and he doesn't want to share me with so many other kids. He's constantly saying I'm unfair."

Sandy continued to share. She had told Joey she would stop running the day care in June. She couldn't stop sooner because of her obligations to the families who counted on her and because she needed the money to support her family. She hadn't figured out how she would earn money when she gave up the day care, but Joey was her primary concern.

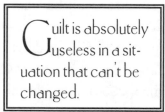

Guilt is absolutely useless in a situation that can't be changed.

The parenting group facilitator asked, "Do you want to give up your day care business?"

Sandy answered with some anger. "No, I love it; but Joey is more important. I want peace and harmony between us, and I worry about his self-esteem."

The facilitator asked, "If there was a way you could keep your day care business and help Joey feel better, would you be interested?"

Sandy didn't hesitate. "Of course I would!"

"Okay, then," said the facilitator. "Let's look at some basics first, then we'll work on some suggestions. Can you give up your day care business without some hidden resentment?"

Sandy thought a moment, "No, probably not. After all, I'm doing this so I can stay home while earning money. I'm doing it for my children, and Joey doesn't understand or appreciate that."

"Who is in control if you give up your day care even when you don't want to?" the facilitator asked.

"Well, obviously Joey is." Sandy shrugged. "I know that isn't healthy, but I can't think what else to do. He obviously needs my attention."

The facilitator continued, "What message are you sending to Joey by allowing him to manipulate you with his emotions?"

Now Sandy smiled wearily. "That he can be a total tyrant—and that's what it feels like to me. I'm so confused. I love him and want to be a good mother, but I will feel resentful if I give in to him and give up a job I love and can do at home. Having a day care program in my home seemed like the perfect way to earn money without having to leave my kids. But the dream has turned into a nightmare."

The facilitator turned to the group. "It's time for some brainstorming. Let's see how many ideas we can come up with that could help Sandy and Joey."

The group came up with a long list of ideas Sandy could try. She was invited to choose the one she would feel most comfortable with. Sandy heard so many good ideas, however, that she chose a combination of several of them:

1. Meet with Joey at a calm time and use the Four Steps for Winning Cooperation. (We'll explain these shortly.)
2. Let Joey have some things that he doesn't have to share with anyone.
3. Spend scheduled, special time with Joey (and with Kyle).
4. Give Joey some jobs so he can feel he's making an important contribution and can also earn some extra money.

5. Get Joey involved in finding solutions to problems so he'll feel he belongs and is significant.
6. Reach out for support by talking to someone in a similar situation who can share his or her experience.

Sandy started with the last suggestion. She called Betty, from the day care association, and shared her problem. Betty laughed and said, "Am I ever glad I'm over that one! I had the same problem when my kids were younger. I think it's very normal. It's hard for kids to share their moms, even when they aren't single moms. Two things helped me. I wouldn't play the 'no fair' game, so my kids didn't hook me with that one. But I did allow them to have toys that were their own and didn't have to be shared with anyone. The other thing was letting them know how much I enjoyed making a good living while still being with them. It helped them to see the benefits as well as the problems."

Sandy was encouraged and relieved to hear that her problem was normal and wasn't happening just because she was a single mom. All kids need attention, but Sandy realized she was loving too much by giving Joey attention in a way that invited unhealthy manipulation. She realized that she had fallen into the trap of trying to "make it up" to her kids because they didn't have a live-in father. It was a relief to give up that belief and all the guilt that went with it.

After talking to Betty, Sandy felt validated for her desire to make a living in a way that included spending time with her kids. Betty had made enough money to stay home with her children and even enough to help put them through college. Betty said, "Of course, there were some problems and some hassles, but what job *doesn't* include some problems? The benefits far outweighed them."

By reaching out for support, Sandy learned the importance of filling her own cup—getting strength and encouragement —before she could fill Joey's cup and resolve the problem. She was able to work with Joey on positive solutions because she was able to drop her misplaced guilt. Now that she was ready, Sandy decided to start with the Four Steps for Winning Cooperation.

The Four Steps for Winning Cooperation
1. **Get into the child's world and make a guess about what he or she might be feeling.** If you're wrong, guess again. (We'll look at getting into your child's world in more depth in chapter 13.)
2. **Show understanding.** Sometimes it helps to describe a time when you felt the same way.
3. **Ask your child whether he or she is willing to listen to your feelings.** Children listen better when they have agreed and when they feel listened to first.
4. **Work on a solution together.** Children are more willing to cooperate in solving problems when they feel understood and listened to.

Sandy was glad to see that Joey was still awake when she finished talking with Betty. Kyle had fallen asleep. It was a perfect time to try the Four Steps for Winning

Cooperation. Sandy started by asking Joey, "Honey, could we have a special talk just between me and you while I'm tucking you into bed?"

"Okay," Joey replied.

Sandy continued, "I was wondering if you feel like you aren't important to me when I'm running the day care."

Sandy had struck a nerve. Joey replied angrily, "It's not fair that I have to share all my stuff."

Sandy concentrated on reflecting and validating his feelings. She offered her understanding and a story of her own. "I can see how you would feel that way. I can re-member when I was a little girl and my mom made me share all my clothes with my younger sister, even my fa-vorites. I hated it. I can see now that by trying to be fair to all the other kids, I was very unfair to you. I made you share your dinnertime chair even when you tried to tell me you didn't think it was fair. I'm so sorry I didn't con-sider your feelings. I'll try to do better from now on."

Joey felt understood. He was touched by his mother's admission and apology, and he started to cry. "I'm sorry for being so bad." Children often cry from relief when they feel understood. When parents take re-sponsibility for disrespectful behavior, children can fol-low their example.

Sandy reassured Joey. "Honey, you aren't bad. We both made some mistakes. I'll bet we can work on some solutions together. First, would you be willing to hear some of my feelings?"

Joey sniffled. "Okay," he said.

Sandy drew Joey close to her. "You're more impor-tant to me than any job. And I'd really like to keep the day care so I don't have to go to work outside our home. I like being able to work and be with you at the same time. Would you be willing to help find some way that we can do this? I know you have some great ideas that I haven't listened to before. I'd really like to hear them now. And maybe you'd like to hear some of mine. Why don't we get a piece of paper and write them down?"

Joey grinned. "Okay!"

Together, Sandy and Joey came up with the following plans: Joey and Sandy would spend fifteen minutes of special time together every day with no phones, no little brother, and no other children. Joey agreed that Kyle should have the same amount of time and that they would all work together during a family meeting on a specific time schedule and what each could do while the other was spending special time with Mom. Joey was enthusiastic about the possibility of helping out and earning some extra money. They agreed that he would earn $2.00 every day by making all the lunches for the day care children. He volunteered to take on other jobs, like picking up toys. They also decided that no one else could sit in his dinner chair unless he gave permission. They ended their talk by agreeing that in the future, if something was bothering them, they would talk about it and work together on solutions that felt respectful to all.

Sandy was ecstatic at her next parenting group. "I can't believe how well this stuff works! Joey is now

> Unlike guilt, regret can serve a purpose if it causes you to study your situation and learn from your mistakes.

helping and seems to feel great about himself instead of misbehaving. At our family meeting, he told Kyle how lucky they are to have a mom who can work at home. When I got Joey involved in problem solving, he had so many good ideas. I'm so glad that I got to tell him how much I love him and that he could really hear me. Thank you all so much!"

Sandy was able to turn a "nightmare" back into a dream. She found a way to use problems as opportunities to learn. Sandy and Joey learned listening skills, problem-solving skills, and cooperation skills. None of this would have happened if Sandy had not discovered how to get out of the win/lose struggle. It wouldn't have been healthy for Joey to "win" at Sandy's expense or for Sandy to "win" at Joey's expense. Control is not an issue when we learn to "win" cooperation *with* our children.

Follow Your Heart

Guilt does not help anyone do his or her best. But guilt can be a cue to examine your feelings and evaluate your decisions. Do you want to work, or do you want to stay home? If you want to stay home, can you? If you want to stay home, follow your heart and do everything possible to create this dream. Tighten your belt; trim your budget; focus on your children instead of material gain. If you need money to survive, find a way to work at home. If you are the type who goes "stir crazy" when you stay home full-time or if you simply must work outside the home, give up your guilt, find *quality* day care, and consider the other suggestions in this book.

Sometimes the emotion we label "guilt" is actually regret. Guilt implies a personal responsibility for your situation, but regret is only sadness that things aren't different—without the emotional pull to "fix" them. You may wish that some of your circumstances could be different. Regret is not pleasant, but unlike guilt, it can serve a purpose if it causes you to study your situation and learn from your mistakes. And you can feel regret and still choose to act in ways that encourage your children to develop sound attitudes and skills. Despite guilt or regret, you can make good decisions about how you will raise the children you love so much, decisions that help them thrive and become the people you hope they will be.

CHAPTER 7

Why Do Parents Keep Doing What Doesn't Work?

By now just about everyone has heard the joke about the definition of insanity—doing the same thing over and over and expecting a different result. This is an apt description for many parenting methods, as one mother discovered when she asked her daughter's school counselor how long she should ground her daughter for refusing to stay grounded the weekend before. However, parents who fail to think about the long-range results of their actions engage in a different kind of insanity—doing things that will produce the opposite of what they hope to achieve with their children. The parenting that has been discussed in previous chapters, what we have called loving too much, does not help children feel loved and does not instill in children the skills and confidence they need to lead happy, productive lives—and usually does not produce better behavior. So why do so many parents keep perpetuating the insanity?

Researchers in universities around the country have completed hundreds of studies on the long-range results of punishment, rewards, and permissiveness. The research proves conclusively that none of these three methods produces positive long-range results with children. So why do well-intentioned, loving parents keep using them? We will explore some possible reasons.

- The research is buried in academic journals that are not read by the general public.
- Parents may lack child development education, parenting education, skills, and just plain common sense about what "works" in the long run to empower children with the perceptions and skills they need for success.
- Parents focus on the behavior instead of on the belief behind the behavior.
- Many parenting "experts" tout the benefits of punishment and rewards.
- A few "experts" promote the benefits of permissiveness.
- Parents believe "I was punished, and I turned out just fine."
- Parents operate from a "crisis mentality": they do what seems to work for the moment without considering the long-range results.
- Parents do what they learned from their parents (or vow to do the opposite).

- Parents become emotionally involved and lose
  their common sense in one of two ways: they react
  in anger, without thinking, when their "buttons"
  get pushed, or they react sympathetically, without
  considering long-range results, when their children are suffering emotionally or physically.

Let's explore in more detail some of the reasons parents continue to do what doesn't work.

Research Is Buried in Academic Journals

Most parents who use punishment (excessive control) or
rewards do so because they believe these methods will
motivate their children to choose better behavior. (We
have discussed the detriments of rescuing and fixing in
previous chapters and will now focus on the detriments
of punishment and rewards.) It would take years to read
all the research that has demonstrated that neither punishment nor rewards are effective motivators for long-
term positive results. Alfie Kohn has summarized much
of this research in *Punished by Rewards* (Houghton
Mifflin, 1993, pp. 42–45), a book we highly recommend.
Kohn describes several research projects that demonstrate how rewards actually impair performance and
how children who tried to earn rewards actually made
more mistakes than those who were simply told the results of their efforts at performing a task.

Praise is a golden calf worshiped by thousands of
"loving" adults who have not investigated the long-

range results. Your own common sense will provide the answer to an important question: Does praise encourage children to appreciate their own self-worth, or does it encourage them to depend on the opinion of others, turning them into "approval junkies"?[1]

Using punishment to manage children's behavior is as problematic as using praise, if not more so. Most parents who punish children usually do so because they truly love those children. They believe punishment will help their children learn better behavior. Again, Kohn eloquently states what we know to be true:

> The unsettling news is that rewards and punishments are worthless at best, and destructive at worst, for helping children develop such values and skills. What rewards and punishment do produce is *temporary compliance.* They buy us obedience. If that's what we mean when we say they "work," then yes, they work wonders. But if we are ultimately concerned with the kind of people our children will become . . . no behavioral manipulation ever helped a child develop a commitment to becoming a caring and responsible person. (p. 160)

What are the long-range results of punishment? Reams of research prove that corporal punishment produces children who are more aggressive than children who do not experience corporal punishment (i.e., good "old-fashioned" spankings). Murray Straus, of the University of New Hampshire Family Research Laboratory, conducted a long-range study that followed families in which spanking was used by "loving" and conscientious

---

1. Kohn takes a much more scientific approach in his chapter "The Praise Problem," taking the time to quote the research and explore, in depth, the long-range negative effects of praise.

parents to manage children's behavior. Straus discovered that *over time* families that relied on spanking and other punishments reported more and more incidences of misbehavior and disrespect in their children. Children who

> Reams of research prove that punishment produces children who are more aggressive than children who do not experience punishment.

were spanked were also more likely to choose violent partners when they became adults. Physical punishment teaches children that violence is an acceptable way to express anger or dissatisfaction to people who are less powerful than you are (Straus, Sugarman, and Giles-Sims, 1997).

Parents Lack Child Development and Parenting Education, Skills, and Common Sense

We often ask parents whether they would consider trying to get a job without an education or training. The answer is "Of course not." Everyone agrees that education and training are necessary, whether the goal is to be a bricklayer or a brain surgeon. We never hear the argument, "Well, my parents didn't get an education or training and it worked for them." (However, we are hearing about a new phenomenon of adult children, raised by parents who loved too much, who are now allowing inherited businesses to fail because they are not willing, or do not know how, to work as hard as their parents did.)

We then ask, "What is the most important job in the world?" All agree that it is parenting. Is it then logical to think that this important job does not require education and training? The problem is that many "parenting experts" provide conflicting information. (This will be discussed in the next section.)

A basic course in child development would help parents avoid some of the typical mistakes of extreme parenting. For example, when parents send their two-year-olds to time-out with the admonition, "Now you just think about what you did," they are motivated to do so by love and the desire to instruct their children. Obviously, the hope is that these two-year-olds will think rationally about what they did, see the errors of their ways, and make a firm commitment to do better.

If these parents had an understanding of basic child development, they would know this is a highly unrealistic expectation for a two-year-old who has not yet reached the age of reason. (Most children younger than the age of three cannot connect cause with effect—or behavior with consequences—in the way that adults can.) Few parents understand this, however, and look chagrined when we ask, "Do you really think you can control what your child is thinking?" It isn't possible to control what people think at any age.

Good parenting education would help these parents get into the world of their two-year-olds to experience what they might be thinking. Because every child is different, there isn't just one possibility. However, it isn't hard to imagine that a child might feel confusion, rebelliousness, or a sense of lowered self-worth. This is not what loving parents want—nor do these feelings encourage a sense of belonging and significance. When parents lack an understanding of child development (or don't use their common sense), they may see only the illusion that time-out seems to stop misbehavior and may fail to consider the long-range consequences.

One father who lacked an understanding of basic child development thought he was doing a loving thing when he took his two and a half–year–old son to a basketball game. (He most likely did not stop to consider whether such a young child would be interested in basketball for any length of time.) Instead of understanding normal behavior for a child that age, he became annoyed when the only thing his son was interested in were the treats that were being hawked up and down the aisles. After listening to his son whine and coax for a few minutes and ordering him to "settle down" and "be quiet," Dad blew up. He grasped the child's hand firmly and proceeded down the wide cement steps at his own pace. The little boy, his face contorted with fear, seemed to be flying as his father dragged him along.

This child couldn't understand what was happening. His "crime" was to be more interested in popcorn and soda than in basketball—a thoroughly appropriate (if irritating) response for a child his age. Although this father loved his son, he failed to understand his little boy's limitations, attempted to control his behavior, lost his own temper, and ultimately frightened his son badly. It is likely to be a long time before this little boy wants to attend another sporting event with dad.

Another father took his family, including a bright two-year-old child, to a drive-in movie. A week later the family drove past the drive-in theater. The two-year-old was bright enough to remember the place and said, "We went there last night." The father said, "It was last week, not last night," stopped the car, and spanked this child because he loved him so much that he didn't want him to grow up to be a liar. It is heartbreaking to consider how often parents' ignorance leads them to punish children for what is simply developmentally appropriate behavior, instead of teaching what children need to learn and celebrating the skills they do have.

Many mistakes made due to a lack of understanding of age-appropriate behavior for children of every age are equally "insane" and heartbreaking. We strongly recommend that every parent take a basic child development class at a community college or read a book on child development.[2]

Parents Focus on the Behavior Instead of on the Belief Behind the Behavior

Human behavior does not occur in a vacuum; there is always a reason why people behave the way they do. Yet most theorists (and parents) look only at behavior

2. Two books that cover child development and how it applies to parenting methods are *Positive Discipline: The First Three Years* and *Positive Discipline for Preschoolers* by Jane Nelsen, Cheryl Erwin, and Roslyn Duffy (Prima, 1999).

(and attempt to change or control it) rather than considering the beliefs *behind* the behavior. It is far easier to change behavior when parents help a child change the perceptions and beliefs that cause that behavior. We can only wonder what decisions the pampered or punished child is making about himself, others, and what he needs to do in life to feel belonging and significance. These decisions usually do not include social interest, a concern for and willingness to contribute to others. Children cannot consider the long-range results of their decisions; parents *must*.

Children's behavior, as we will learn in future chapters, is a sort of "code" for what they believe about themselves and others. They "act out" their needs and beliefs. If children are demanding undue attention or using misguided power, wise parents will give their children experiences that lead to different decisions, helping them find a feeling of belonging and significance in positive, appropriate ways. For example, a child demanding undue attention will be given opportunities to get useful attention through tasks that are helpful to the family, such as bringing the diapers, helping with dinner (even toddlers can tear lettuce and scramble eggs, with supervision), or doing any task that leads to a sense of contribution. The key is to be aware of the decisions children are making because that is what shapes their personality.

Alfred Adler, in *The Problem Child* (Capricorn, 1963), agreed with most child development theorists that a child's personality ("life style") is shaped by the age of four to five years old but differs in *how* it is shaped. Adler stated, "Heredity and environment are only the building blocks which an individual uses for constructing (through his interpretations and decisions about his experiences) his unique way of fitting himself into life as he finds it" (p. iv). When describing the *problem child*, Adler stated, "Spoiled children constitute a great segment of the population. I do not believe I am exaggerating when I say that from fifty to sixty percent of all children have been made dependent" (p. xv).

It is amazing how many four-year-olds have already developed the belief "I'm the boss of my house." Adlerian psychologists have discovered this over and over through a method called *goal disclosure.* When a child is using misguided power to engage parents in power struggles, an Adlerian psychologist will ask, "Could it be that you do this to get your parents to notice you and pay attention to you?" If the mistaken goal of behavior was undue attention, the child might get a big grin on his face while saying no. This is called a *recognition reflex,* which means the child's "subconscious" goal has just been revealed. If the mistaken goal is not undue attention, however, the child will most likely say no without the grin.

The Adlerian then goes on to the next question: "Could it be that you do this behavior to let your parents know that you are the boss or that no one can tell you what to do?" Again, the child may say no while grinning reflexively. In a recent demonstration, a delightful four-year-old did not bother to deny it. She said, with a huge smile, "Yes, I'm the boss." The parents were then advised to start giving their daughter opportunities to use her power in useful ways, such as participating in family meetings where she could use her intelligence to brainstorm for solutions to problems and make some different decisions about how to find belonging and significance. Caring parents will consider the decisions their children might be making in response to the parenting methods taught by "experts."

Many Parenting "Experts" Tout the Benefits of Punishment and Rewards

Magazine articles and books are filled with advice from "parenting experts" who advocate punishment and rewards, usually in the name of loving parenting. Their intentions are admirable. There is not one "expert" that says, "Do not love your children." Those who advocate punishment truly believe it is the best way to help children learn good behavior. Either they haven't read the research on the detriments of punishment, or they don't believe it.

Throughout this book, we encourage parents to educate themselves about research, different methods, and child development, and then to use their common sense and wisdom to get into their child's world and investigate the long-range results of what they do. Your children are exactly that: *your* children. You know them better than anyone else can, and you must ultimately decide what decisions you want them to make about what "works" in life. You will be able to do this important task far better when you have enough knowledge to understand development and behavior *and* to trust your own wisdom and common sense.

In *Childhood and Society* (Norton, 1963), Erik Erikson developed a theory of social and psychological development that is widely accepted by those who have studied child development. He proposed that the first year of life is the window for the development of a sense of trust versus mistrust. It is our opinion that this theory is misunderstood by the advocates of permissiveness.[3]

Erikson taught that infants must have their basic needs met if they are to develop a sense of trust instead of a sense of mistrust. The problem occurs when parents and experts follow a misguided definition of needs that includes "wants" as well as needs.

A Few "Experts" Promote the Benefits of Permissiveness

Advocates of attachment parenting (as taught by Dr. William Sears) believe in sharing the family bed, responding to every whimper, wearing the baby in a sling or carrying him constantly, or having one parent stay home to respond to the child's every need. Parents who practice this approach to child rearing often rush to soothe a fussing child when this child might be better served (after being diapered, fed, and hugged) by faith in her abilities to self-soothe.

Most people think they would just love to have someone give them everything they want and take care

---

3. It is important to note that many experts, such as Dr. Benjamin Spock, have been accused of advocating permissiveness because they do not believe in punishment. This is a gross error. Dr. Spock never advocated permissiveness yet is often accused of teaching parents to spoil children.

of every problem for them. Yet, would that really serve their best interests? In such a world, how would people develop competency skills and self-confidence? We believe children may not develop trust when every want is met; instead they may develop mistrust in themselves and dependence on others.

Take the issue of children sleeping in their parents' beds. There are many cultures where the family bed is a cultural norm. This situation creates a family atmosphere that is much different from situations in which parents do not want their children in their beds and engage in many power struggles before giving in. Children of parents who choose the "family bed" with confidence are more likely to develop confidence than are children of parents who end up with children in their bed by default instead of by choice. Erik Erickson theorized that parental confidence is one of the primary factors in helping children develop confidence.

Extremism and Separate Realities

Whether parenting experts advocate permissiveness or control, most seem to demonstrate a sad lack of respect for other opinions. Followers of Dr. William Sears, who believe in attachment parenting, make insulting claims about other kinds of parenting. Those who do not believe in attachment parenting denigrate those who do. Each group believes they are parenting in the most effective way, while each may be parenting in ineffective, even damaging ways. One may be going to the extreme of overindulgence. The other may be going to the extreme of excessive control. What do these opposing groups have to say about each other?

Claims of attachment parenting advocates. Those who favor "attachment parenting" claim that anything else is *detachment* parenting and "builds distance between parent and child, particularly by setting the two up as opponents and by encouraging holding back on natural, loving, instinctive responses."[4] They cite as evidence the many less-developed cultures in the world that practice instinctive forms of "attachment parenting" (or earlier times when limitations in space and resources dictated that families sleep together) and claim that these should be our role models.

Children do not develop trust when every want is met.

Claims of advocates of excessive control. Those who preach the doctrine of control and "authority" insist that children will be spoiled and self-centered if parents meet every demand. Children who are indulged will grow up thinking "the world owes them a living." Indulged children lead their parents around as though they had rings in their noses. Gary Esso and Robert Buchnam, in their book *On Becoming Babywise* (Mulrnomah, 1998), teach that infants should be fed on a

---

4. See http://www.ozemail.com.au/~chriskaz/attachparent/attachparent.html

strict schedule (whether they're hungry or not) rather than on demand and that there's nothing wrong with spanking a toddler until it stings.

The truth lies somewhere in the middle. Just plain common sense would tell most people that healthy loving lies somewhere in the middle of these extremes. Babies can be loved, held, and even nursed on demand without going to the extreme of sleeping with them and carrying them around constantly. Most toddlers can develop security and social interest through routines that are respectful of everyone concerned, but far short of the rigid routines recommended by Esso and Buchnam. Sears believes that crying is a child's only way to communicate. Esso and Buchnam believe that babies cry to manipulate their parents. Could it be that the truth is somewhere in the middle—that at times a child is crying to communicate hunger, wetness, or simply the need to be held and that at other times it is an expression of his need to practice self-soothing? (Of course, when parents jump in too soon, the child usually learns the art of manipulation instead of the skill of self-soothing.).

> Parents can use the knowledge they gain from child development, research, and parenting education to follow their hearts instead of following extremism in either direction.

Parents who tune in to both possibilities seem to know when the cries of their children indicate genuine needs. They also know when they feel manipulated. They use the knowledge they gain from child development, research, and parenting education to follow their hearts instead of following extremism in either direction. They also tune in to their children and watch their actions to become aware of the decisions their children might be making about how to find belonging and significance. Wise parents learn to ask, "If I do this, what will my child learn and decide?" Intimate knowledge of a child's personality and temperament, familiarity with age-appropriate behavior, and common sense help these parents evaluate the long-term effectiveness of their parenting decisions. This is the foundation of healthy loving.

Often, after parents have been presented with all the evidence against punishment and permissiveness, and after they have been encouraged to "think" about the long-range results of what they are doing, they offer another argument.

"I Was Punished, and I Turned Out Just Fine"

How fine is "fine"? Fine is relative. Yes, most of us turned out just "fine." We can even laugh at some of the punishments we received as children—and even say we deserved it. However, if we had been allowed to learn from our mistakes instead of being made to pay for them, is it possible we might be even better than "fine"?

Stan told his parenting group about a time he cheated on a fifth-grade test. He said, "I was stupid enough to write some answers on the palm of my hand. The teacher saw me open my fist to find an answer."

This teacher grabbed Stan's paper and, in front of everyone in the class, tore it up. He received an F on the test and was publicly called a "cheater." The teacher told his parents. His father gave him a whipping and grounded him for a month. Stan said, "I never cheated again, and I certainly deserved the F."

The group leader helped him explore this experience to help everyone in the class see if there might be a more productive way to handle this situation.

Leader: Does everyone agree with Stan that he deserved the F?

Group: Yes.

Leader: Would that have been enough to teach him the consequences of his choices, or did he need the punishment also?

Group: Hmmmmm.

Leader: What do you think, Stan? How did you feel about getting the F for cheating?

Stan: I felt very guilty and very embarrassed.

Leader: What did you decide from that?

Stan: That I wouldn't do it again.

Leader: What did you decide after receiving the punishment?

Stan: That I was a disappointment to my parents. I still worry about disappointing them.

Leader: So how did the punishment help you?

Stan: Well, I had already decided I wouldn't cheat again. The guilt and embarrassment of that was enough to teach me that lesson. Actually, the worry about disappointing my parents is a real burden.

Leader: If you had a magic wand and could change the script of that event, how would you change it? How would you change what anyone said or did?

Stan: Well, I wouldn't cheat.

Leader: And after that?

Stan: I don't know.

Leader: Who has any ideas for Stan? It is usually easier to see possibilities when you aren't emotionally involved. What could Stan's teacher or parents have done or said that would have demonstrated healthy loving?

Group Member: I'm a teacher, and I'm learning a lot from this. The teacher could have taken Stan aside and asked him why he was cheating.

Leader: Stan, what would you have answered to that?

Stan: That I wanted to pass the test.

Group Member: Then I could appreciate his desire to pass and ask him how he felt about cheating as a way to accomplish that.

Stan: I would promise never to do it again.

Group Member: I would then tell him he would have to receive an F for this test but that I was glad he had learned to avoid cheating. I would then ask him to prepare a plan for me about what he would do to pass the next test.

Stan: I would still feel guilty and embarrassed about cheating, but I would also appreciate the kindness along with the firmness. Now I see what that means.

Leader: Now do you have any ideas how you could use your magic wand to change what your parents did?

Stan: It would be nice if they had acknowledged how guilty and embarrassed I felt. They could have empathized about what a tough lesson that was for me to learn. Then they could express their faith in me to learn from my experience and to do the right thing in the future. They could reassure me that they would love me no matter what, but that they hoped I wouldn't disappoint myself in the future. Wow, what a concept—to worry more about disappointing myself than my parents. I find that very encouraging.

Several points are made by this discussion about healthy loving:

1. Healthy love does not mean letting children "get away" with their behavior.
2. Healthy love does mean helping children explore the consequences of their choices in a supportive environment so that lasting growth and learning can take place.
3. Most people turned out "fine" even if they were punished—but they might have learned even more had they received unconditional love and both kindness and firmness to learn from mistakes.

Turning out "fine" isn't the issue. There is always room for improvement. This world of ours has not stood still, and as we have discovered, families and children have changed and evolved. Parents, too, must evolve and find methods that are more effective than those that have been used in the past. Parents who love in healthy ways are not satisfied with "fine." They want to give their children the kind of nurturing that helps them "bloom" into the best people they can possibly be.

Parents Operate from a "Crisis Mentality"

There is another reason why parents so often continue to do what doesn't work. They find themselves dealing with one crisis after another, reacting the best way they can. For instance, parents pamper and give in to their children (or punish them) because it seems to work at the moment. After all, most children do stop crying (or stop misbehaving for the moment) when parents pamper or punish. The subtle difficulty, as we have learned, is that what works for the moment often does not teach children what parents truly want them to learn. "Crisis thinking" tempts parents into reacting without considering the long-range results, the decisions their children are making, and how those decisions will affect future behavior.

Parents Do What They Learned from Their Parents (or Vow to Do the Opposite)

We will examine this issue in depth in chapter 11. Most people either liked or disliked the way they were raised. If they liked it, they may want to repeat what their parents did—even if it was ultimately unhealthy. Even more compelling are the feelings of those who did not like how they were raised. Too many parents have vowed that they wouldn't do to their kids what was done to them. The problem is that they often choose an opposite extreme. If their parents were too strict, they are likely to be too lenient. Extremes are rarely healthy for children.

Reprinted with special permission by King Features Syndicate.

Parents Become Emotionally Involved and Lose Their Common Sense

Love is a powerful emotion and motivates a great deal of human behavior. As we have mentioned many times, it is also one of the primary reasons parents keep doing what doesn't work. Emotional involvement usually takes one of two extremes.

First, parents might react in anger, without thinking, when their "buttons" get pushed. Parents have buttons, and children know what they are and how to push them. It's when their buttons are pushed that parents revert to their primitive brain (fight or flight) and "lose it." Everything they know (and the actions they would most likely choose when calm) evaporates into the ether. The primitive brain is sometimes referred to as the *reptilian brain*. (It is sobering to remember that many reptiles eat their young.) While in this state of mind, parents usually go on a rampage that puts children into the same state of mind. When the only options are fight or flight, parents and children plunge into the war zone.

Power struggles between adults and children seem to be epidemic.

Awareness of this phenomenon can help. Parents can learn (and can teach their children) that this is time for some "positive time-out"[5] until the rational brain can be accessed again. Parents can also learn how to disconnect their emotional "buttons." Some common buttons children push are "But all the other kids get to do it," "You're not fair," or "I hate you." Buttons can also be nonverbal: ask any parent whose teen has rolled her eyes once too often or flipped dad "the bird." When parents can learn not to react to button pushing, children eventually stop trying (well, most of the time anyway!).

Second, parents may react sympathetically, without considering long-range results, when their children are suffering emotionally or physically. Parents never enjoy watching their children suffer, even when the suffering can be a valuable life lesson (remember the butterfly emerging from the chrysalis?). Healthy parenting involves empathy without rescuing. Hugs or validating a child's feelings with reflective listening will go a long way in helping children learn from their experiences without overprotecting them. Remember, children have an inherent ability to self-soothe and to learn from their own experiences. Undeniably, it is difficult for you when your child is sad, lonely, or anxious, but respectful support (rather than sympathetic rescue attempts) is usually a more effective—and ultimately more loving—response.

---

5. See Jane Nelsen, *Positive Time Out and 50 Other Ways to Avoid Power Struggles in Homes and Classrooms* (Prima, 1999).

Many parents assume that making the right decisions will always feel good, but sometimes being a truly loving and effective parent is tough work.

We have discussed formal research. Our own research comes from practical experience, which you can duplicate with your own children. Punishment and rewards simply do not work *over the long term* and do not represent healthy loving, nor do they encourage conscientious change and growth. (If you need further evidence, consider the results currently being produced by our criminal and juvenile justice systems.) We often say, "Beware of what works," because it is true that both punishment and reward seem to work for short-term benefits. We all know children who have promised to be quiet in the grocery story when told they will be rewarded with a candy bar at the checkout stand. We know of children who have stopped their misbehavior (for the moment) when punished. However, most adults fail to explore the long-range results of these tactics and continue to use them "in the name of love."

If you take the time to get into the child's world and explore what that child is thinking, feeling, and deciding while receiving rewards and punishment, you will see how pointless these methods are. The child who receives a candy bar for being quiet is most likely receiving a powerful lesson in blackmailing techniques. The child who is punished is most likely deciding to go along when others are more powerful, to rebel, or to avoid getting caught whenever possible.

At one of our parenting workshops, where we discuss the long-range negative results of punishment and rewards, a participant named Karen refused to believe that these tactics were not beneficial. Karen had received her doctorate at a university that favored behaviorism (the use of punishment and rewards as primary motivators).[6] She had spent years of her life and a lot of money learning that behaviorism was the best way to motivate people.

At the workshop, Karen volunteered to role-play a child during an activity on the long-range results of rewards. During the role-play, she was offered M&M's and gold stars (with a big reward after filling her chart with gold stars) to make her bed in the morning. To help adults understand the world of children, the final phase of the activity is to ask, "What are you thinking, feeling, and deciding in your role as the child?" Before we even finished the role-play, Karen threw up her hands and said, "I get it. As the child, I'm sitting here trying to figure out how I can get a bigger reward

> Punishment and rewards simply do not work *over the long term* and do not represent healthy loving, nor do they encourage conscientious change and growth.

or how I can gain power by refusing to do it in spite of their rewards. I might do it this time, but I'm more interested in what I'll get than in self-improvement. I can't believe this."

In *Punished by Rewards,* Alfie Kohn makes an interesting statement about B. F. Skinner, who was responsible

---

6. See B. F. Skinner, *Beyond Freedom and Dignity* (New York: Knopf, 1971); J. B. Watson, *Behaviorism* (New York: Norton, 1924).

for the popularization of behaviorism: "B. F. Skinner could be described as a man who conducted most of his experiments on rodents and pigeons and wrote most of his books about people" (p. 6). Children are most definitely *people* and deserve to learn about life and how to live it with respect and dignity.

This brings us back to the basic question asked in the title of this chapter: Why do parents, who unquestionably love their children, keep doing what doesn't work? Sometimes we wonder whether parents truly *think*. Lest you think we are being judgmental, we want to make it clear that we have participated in this state of nonthinking ourselves—many times over. Thoughtful consideration and experience, however, have helped us arrive at different conclusions. How grateful we are that mistakes truly are opportunities to learn! All parents must learn to think seriously about what it means to love in healthy ways—and to act on what they discover.

Good Parents Still Make Mistakes

It is important to repeat that it isn't "bad parents" who praise, punish, or pamper. Surveys have shown that 80 percent of parents—most of them loving and committed—spank their children. Some feel very righteous about this fact, while others would prefer another alternative but just don't know what it might be. They certainly don't want to be permissive, which is often thought of as the only alternative. Many people see things as "black or white" without seeing the many shades in between. These "shades" are often seen as "wishy-washy" instead of truly better alternatives.

Parents who feel righteous about spanking follow the admonition to "spare the rod and spoil the child." But the Bible tells us, "Thy rod and Thy staff, they comfort me" (Psalm 23: 4). Biblical scholars know that the rod was used as a guide to provide safe boundaries, not as a tool for beating or hitting. Children cannot be driven; they can only be led. The Bible also tells us that God is our loving Father, a Father who recognizes that His children have free will and will sometimes choose wrong behavior. The Bible has far more to say about honor, respect, teaching, and love than it does about punishment.

> Hugs or validating children's feelings with active listening go a long way in helping them learn from their experiences without overprotecting them.

We receive many questions from parents asking for help. They often say, "I have tried everything." When we ask them to list what they have tried, they list punishment after punishment: spanking, yelling, threatening, grounding, taking away toys, and punitive time-out (as opposed to positive time-out). But few parents enjoy punishing their children. When they are offered different tools, ones that teach good judgment and encourage appropriate behavior without the yelling and shame that seem to accompany "discipline" in so many families, they are both hopeful and truly relieved.

Parents who punish, and parents who use rewards and praise, do so because they love their children.

Healthy loving, however, considers the long-range results of discipline. Parents who practice healthy loving have an understanding that discipline and punishment are not synonymous. In later chapters, we continue to explore healthy discipline and the tools that accomplish it. For now, if you're beginning to think that the ways you've been parenting your children aren't working well—for you or for them—and may not produce the long-term results you want, stop doing what isn't working, consider some new ideas, and trust your wisdom and common sense to help you learn to love in effective ways.

CHAPTER 8

The Essential
(and Uncomfortable)
Process of Weaning

Every animal in the animal kingdom, except humans, knows the importance of weaning. They instinctively know that young animals will not become adult animals (and won't survive long as adults should they be lucky enough to make it that far) unless they are weaned.

Mother animals are not influenced at all by the fact that their offspring do not enjoy the weaning process (actually, the mothers don't enjoy it much, either). Have you ever watched a young animal try to nurse after its mother has decided it is time to wean? Every time a colt or calf tries to suckle, the mother animal uses her head to butt him away. It does not matter how hard the young animal tries; the mother knows that weaning is essential to self-reliance and survival.

Differences and Similarities

Yes, humans are different from the rest of the animal kingdom, but there are some similarities. The similarities are that human children also need to be weaned to develop the self-reliance that will help them survive more successfully in society. The weaning isn't only from the breast or bottle (although most mothers can tell you that process can be tough enough); human parents must wean their children—gradually and lovingly—from emotional and physical dependence.

A primary difference between animal mothers and human mothers is that humans sometimes allow their emotions to take precedence over the long-term good of their children. A human mother tries to wean her child. The child cries. The mother can't stand it, so she gives in. This mother has just made a huge mistake in the name of love. She has loved her child "too much" to let that child suffer for the moment—and has just insured greater suffering (for both of them) later on.

> A primary difference between animal and human mothers is that humans sometimes allow emotions to take precedence over the long-term good of their children.

Remember, we are talking about much more than weaning infants from the breast or bottle. However, it is interesting to note that for most infants there is a window of time during which they are ready to be weaned from the breast or bottle. Mothers often miss or even ignore this window (a time when infants try to refuse the bottle or breast) for a variety of reasons: they want their child to continue to nurse, or a bottle comforts him at night, or it is easier to provide this method of comfort to a child. When the time nature has decreed for weaning is missed, the process is almost always made harder for both mother and child. The breast or bottle soon becomes a habit or a "want" instead of a need.

Too often human mothers (and fathers) give their children what they want instead of what they need. Loving parents would be unlikely to do this if they understood that they were hurting their children instead of helping them. Here is a list of just a few of the things that children want, followed by a list of what they actually need:

Wants	Needs
Mommy to help me get to sleep	To learn to go to sleep by myself
To sleep in Mommy's bed	To sleep in my own bed
To dress me	Teach me to dress myself and then don't give in and do it for me
Every toy I see on TV and in the store	To empathize with my feelings while not giving in, and to show me how I can earn and save money to buy my own
Mommy and Daddy to solve my problems	To learn to solve my own problems (with support from Mommy and Daddy)

Wants	*Needs*
Mommy and Daddy to protect me from experiencing problems or being upset	Mommy and Daddy to have faith in me to handle and survive problems
To rescue me when I make financial mistakes	To show empathy while brainstorming with me about what I learned and how I can fix it
To buy me a car	Help me figure out how to buy my own car
To rescue me when I can't make car insurance payments	To hold my car keys until I can make the insurance payments again
To let me do whatever I want	To work with me on setting limits that are respectful to all concerned
No lectures, blame, shame, or punishment	No lectures, blame, shame or punishment, but respectful discussions (family meetings or one-to-one) for joint problem solving
To borrow money	To have a good track record of repayment or to hear (in a kind but firm voice) no

How Are Children Hurt When Parents Avoid Weaning?

You might believe that failing to wean in the name of love is a modern phenomenon, but consider the story of Hazel. Hazel is 94 years old. She grew up on a farm on the plains of Alberta, Canada; she was the only one of three siblings to survive infancy and was, not surprisingly, precious to her hardworking parents. Life on an isolated farm was difficult for a couple with no sons and a young daughter, so eventually Hazel's father gave up the farm and moved to a small town to work. In fact, the family moved several times, never quite finding prosperity.

Hazel was exceedingly lovely. Her friends and neighbors told her that she looked just like Mary Pickford, and she was the undisputed belle of the dances held each weekend at the local hall. The boys all fought over Hazel, but she (and her doting father) eventually selected Albert to court her. When they married, caring for Hazel became Albert's responsibility, and he took that responsibility seriously indeed.

Albert and Hazel eventually moved to California in search of a better life. Albert worked very hard; Hazel took care of their home and raised their daughter, Katherine. Albert adored his lovely wife and wanted to spare her as much of the stress and drudgery of life as possible; he took over just where her father had left off. Hazel never learned to handle money, drive a car, or pay bills. She couldn't write a check or make even small repairs to the home. Albert handled everything. As Hazel and Albert aged, Albert managed her medical care and dispensed her medications for her. In addition, Albert made sure Katherine knew that caring for Hazel would eventually become her responsibility. "Take care of your mother when I'm gone," he told her repeatedly.

Albert was 88 when he passed away. Hazel was devastated by grief, and as time went on, Katherine realized that her mother wasn't really recovering. And that wasn't all: Hazel was completely helpless. She could do nothing for herself. Although her daughter tried to teach her to write a check and to pay her bills, Hazel claimed she "couldn't." Eventually Katherine stopped trying to teach her. Nothing satisfied Hazel, either; she missed Albert and no matter what her daughter did for her, how often she called and visited, or how caring she tried to be, Hazel was unhappy. She complained. She found fault with everything. She failed to recognize that Katherine had a family of her own to care for. And she wondered why her family didn't rush to spend time with her.

Hazel had been loved so much that she lost not only the ability to care for herself but her ability to appreciate the gifts and blessings she enjoyed. Hazel is living a long—and unhappy—life because those around her loved her too much.

But Don't Children Need to Be Taken Care Of?

Of course, it is certainly the parents' job to take care of their children, but what is the best way to do that? Parents will do the best job when they take time to consider the long-range results of their care (as we have said over and over). In chapter 2, we discussed how children are always making decisions about themselves, others, the world, and what they must do to thrive or to survive. Parents need to consider the decisions children make when they are weaned—and the decisions they make when they are not weaned. Let's take a look at that common family battleground, getting dressed in the morning.

During our parenting lectures we often ask parents, "At what age are children capable of dressing themselves?" It is amazing how many loving parents believe children can't do this task until they are four or five. We happen to know, from our own experience and the experience of many other parents, that children are quite capable of dressing themselves from the time they are two years old—if parents take time for training, if they establish a consistent routine, and if they buy the kind of clothing that is easy to pull over or slip on. (Fancy buckles, buttons, and bows are too difficult for small children because their fine-motor skills are not yet fully developed.)

We then ask, "Why do you think your neighbors are still dressing their children—because we know none of you would rob your children of the feelings of capability they have when they dress themselves?" After laughing at the joke, parents admit that there are two main reasons they are still dressing their children when they are old enough to do it themselves:

1. It is more expedient—faster and easier.
2. Children look better. (Who hasn't cringed at the appearance of a proud and happy toddler clad in red pants, an orange shirt—backward, of course—and shoes on the wrong feet? Instead of a return trip to the bedroom, celebrate your child's very real accomplishment—and take a photograph for posterity.)

Of course, there is another reason. Once children become used to having you dress them, they may insist that you continue this maid service and whine, cry, or just plain stall until you do it. We encourage parents to tell their neighbors (or each other) that, for the sake of expediency and looking good for others, they are robbing their children of the opportunity to believe that they are capable and can be contributing members of their family.

Think about it. What decisions are children likely to make when their parents dress them when they are capable of dressing themselves? Consider these possibilities: "I'm not capable." "Love means getting others to take care of me." "I deserve special service." "I can use this situation to get undue attention or to use my power to get others to do what I want." We can't think of any healthy decisions that children might make from being served and waited on. Can you?

If you have been dressing your children and you now see that it is not the most loving thing you can do for them, there is one more catch: Do you think it will be easy to stop?

Weaning Is Never Easy for the Weanee or the Weanor

It is easy to understand why weaning is not easy for children. But why is it so difficult for parents? Why is it so difficult to grasp the fact that weaning is beneficial to children even when they don't like it at the time? (They will thank you for it later, we promise.)

It usually comes back to emotions. Remember, doing the right thing doesn't always *feel* good at the moment. Parents don't want their children to suffer, and they don't want to suffer themselves. Angry children may stomp their feet; they may even say, "I hate you." They may *believe* they hate you. However, if weaning is done in a kind and firm manner, we can promise you that the reverse is true.

The unfortunate paradox in loving children so much that you fail to wean them is that children inevitably resent you for it later on. Haven't you noticed that the more you do for children and the more you give them, the more they want and demand? Parents really think their

> In most cases, if you feel that you are being manipulated, you are.

children will appreciate all they do for them and are continually hurt and disappointed when they see their children becoming spoiled brats instead of grateful. The reverse, fortunately, is also true: children will respect and appreciate you (eventually) when you love them enough to wean them and teach them self-confidence and self-reliance—if you use the magic keys for weaning.

Magic Keys for Successful Weaning
1. Expect to feel uncomfortable.
2. Do what is right with kindness and firmness at the same time.

Expect to Feel Uncomfortable

It may not make sense to you that loving in healthy ways is sometimes very uncomfortable, but this is a very important concept to grasp. It is much more comfortable to rescue children, give in to them, or help them feel better when they are upset. We repeat: Weaning is never comfortable for the weanee or the weanor, but weaning is essential to healthy growth and development. If what you are doing in the process of weaning your child *feels* good, it may be an unhealthy thing to do. If it feels uncomfortable, it just may be the most loving thing you can do for your child.

For example, it may feel very uncomfortable for you to say No. After all, your child will be unhappy if he can't have that toy. It may feel very uncomfortable to hear your child cry while learning to fall asleep by herself. You may be afraid that she is feeling unloved instead of knowing she is learning self-reliance and faith in herself.

It is important to note once again that we are not talking about abandoning children or ignoring their safety, health, or genuine fears. There is a simple way to know whether your child is trying to manipulate you: If you feel manipulated, you are! And feeling manipulated is solid evidence that it's time to begin the weaning process.

When your children get older, it is very uncomfortable to have them think you are the meanest parent in the world. ("All the *other* kids get to do it! You never let me do *any*thing!") You may fear that the only way to keep your children's love is to give in and do whatever they want. But think about that for a minute. Is real love based only on "getting what I want"?

> If what you are doing in the process of weaning your child *feels* good, it may be an unhealthy thing to do.

Do What Is Right with Kindness and Firmness at the Same Time

You may have heard the phrase "attitude is everything." Like it or not, these words apply to parenting as well. Even the wisest actions done with an attitude of shaming or humiliation will fail to have the desired effect. Many parents lack the courage to do what is right (weaning) without using blame, shame, and pain in the form of lectures, martyrdom, or punishment. See whether you recognize any of these lectures: "Do you think I'm made of money?" "You are so selfish. Do you think the world revolves around you?" "Can't you ever take no for an answer?" "After all I have done for you, all you want is more, more, more!"

Parents should listen to their own lectures from time to time. Why would a child believe you are made of

Calvin and Hobbes

money unless you have given them that impression? Why shouldn't they be selfish when they get everything they want? Why wouldn't they think the world revolves around them when it usually does? How can they learn to take no for an answer when they don't get any practice at it? Why wouldn't they want more, more, more? If you haven't heard the news, here is the bulletin: The more you do for children, the more they expect—and the less capable and confident they become. Does it surprise you that instead of feeling gratitude, children just want more? What other decisions could they make about themselves, others, the world, and what to do, based on the experiences you are giving them?

When you are kind and firm at the same time, you and your children may feel uncomfortable at first. Your children may even be genuinely unhappy. But you will both feel better later on. Unless you are unkind and disrespectful, they will not hate you (forever) and they won't hold on to their anger forever. However, if you have been intentionally unkind, you will feel guilty and your children may have reason to hate you. Then, because of your guilt, you may give in to their demands to regain their love, thus creating a vicious cycle.

The longer weaning has been delayed, the more uncomfortable everyone will feel and the longer your children may hold on to their anger. When you respect the needs of the situation (that your children will not learn self-reliance unless weaned) and do what is right with kindness and firmness, your children will eventually learn to respect both you and themselves.

Temper Tantrums

Q: I have a beautiful five-month-old son who started about two weeks ago to have temper tantrums. He yells so hard that sometimes he stops breathing for a moment. I try to keep him busy with toys, sing-alongs, and so forth, but it's not working; he gets bored fast and yells again. I think it might be because he's teething, but I'm afraid he'll get used to doing these temper tantrums to get what he wants since every time he yells I go to him. I've tried to let him yell a for a little while before I go to him now, but he just yells louder and then starts crying. I need help; I don't know what to do. I'm not in favor of spanking, but I'm not sure he understands when I tell him not to yell because he starts laughing when I pick him up.

A. We don't know for sure if it is teething, but from what we read in your question, it sounds as though he is training you well. As the mothers of eight (between us), we know how difficult it is to find the balance between giving needed comfort and going to an extreme that teaches manipulation. It is especially difficult at this age. Few things are more heartbreaking than deciding to let a child cry it out and then learning that he has a fever.

Given all of that, trying to find the balance between providing needed comfort and teaching manipulation is important to both you and your son. It is not good to train him to be a manipulator, and you will end up feeling very resentful. Also, he cannot learn that he is capable and that he can handle minor upsets and disappointments on his own when you rush in to rescue him.

So, how do you find the balance? Listen to your intuition. In most cases, if you feel that you are being manipulated, you are. However, spanking is never the answer. If you have trained him to be manipulative, it is up to you to train him (in a kind and firm way) that this is no longer acceptable. Weaning is never easy for the weanor or the weanee, so don't expect this to be easy. Often, what is easiest at the moment is not the best thing to do for long-term effective results: teaching self-reliance, confidence, and cooperation.

We suggest that once you have given your son some loving attention, and you know that he is not hungry, tired, or wet, allow him to have his feelings—which may be expressed by screaming. Of course, he won't understand when you tell him not to yell. He is not developmentally able to understand such a concept. However, children at this age do seem to understand actions much better than words. If it doesn't work to get your attention by screaming, he will eventually stop doing that. We must warn you, however, that inconsistency can be dangerous. You're likely to get more screaming if you ignore him sometimes and give in at other times. It is most effective when you have confidence that you are doing the right thing for both of you—even when it is not easy. Far too many parents do what is easy at the moment instead of what is effective for the long term.

We would like to leave you with an encouraging example that was shared with us. "I'll never forget the time I was dealing with a child who was having temper tantrums. I had decided to try ignoring them, but wasn't sure that was the right thing to do. My mother was visiting at the time. Mom asked me where she could find a needle. My son was lying on the floor having one of his fits. She stepped over my son without missing a beat and said, 'Where did you say those needles are?' She did not pay any attention to my screaming son and in her wonderful way let me know that what I was doing was just fine and that I need not feel guilty. As you might guess, my son grew up to be a wonderful young man and a loving father who does not feel deprived or unloved because I didn't cater to his every demand."

A Case Study

Yolanda loved her children so much that she had difficulty saying no. (Of course, she had some other issues such as a lifestyle priority that told her people wouldn't love her if she didn't give in to them and "please" them; more about that in chapter 12.) She continued to follow this pattern long after her children had become adults. One of her daughters, Beverly, became the manager for Yolanda's successful business. When Beverly needed money, Yolanda loaned her money, including the down payment on a house Yolanda knew Beverly and her husband couldn't really afford. But what mother doesn't want her daughter to have a good life?

> Unless you are unkind and disrespectful, your children will not hate you (forever) and they won't hold on to their anger forever.

The day came when Yolanda, Beverly, and her husband Sal sat down and went over the figures together. Yolanda and Sal could see that the monthly payments and maintenance for such a luxurious home would be too expensive for Beverly and Sal. But Beverly promised to scrimp and save and go without so they could afford the house. Yolanda and Sal knew that it just wouldn't work, but when Beverly left the room in tears, Yolanda couldn't stand it. Neither could Sal. And so they gave in.

It wasn't long before Beverly and Sal's inevitable financial problems caused serious conflict in their marriage. Yolanda felt terrible when she realized she had hurt them more than helped them by giving in because she couldn't stand to see Beverly's tears. She realized she had to say no when Beverly asked for more money.

Beverly was not used to hearing no from her mother, so she embezzled money from Yolanda's company. She wrote checks to cover a mortgage payment and some furniture for the home. The scrimping and saving lasted about a month before Beverly started using credit cards to get the things she wanted.

When Yolanda did the accounting and discovered the checks that Beverly had written, she was devastated. She felt betrayed. How could Beverly do such a thing after all she had done for her? Still, Yolanda was ready to give Beverly another chance if she promised she would never do it again.

Yolanda was so upset that she sought the help of a therapist who helped her understand that she was making another mistake in the name of love. The therapist helped her see that she was creating weakness in Beverly instead of helping her. Yolanda discovered to her dismay that doing the right thing was going to be agonizingly difficult. But her very real love for her daughter guided Yolanda to see what she needed to do.

Yolanda called Beverly and was both kind and firm while telling her, "Everyone makes mistakes and that is okay. We simply need to correct the mistakes. You made a mistake by embezzling the money. I made a mistake by saying you could have another chance before you corrected your mistake. I will always love you, and I am willing to give you another chance—after you have repaid what you stole. When you repay the money, I will be happy to have you work for the company again. Meanwhile, you will need to find another job until you correct this mistake."

Beverly objected, "But how can I pay you back if you fire me?"

Yolanda said, "I'm asking you to take an unpaid leave until the money is paid back. I have faith that you will find a way to solve this problem. I hope you will want to work in the business again, but that will be your choice." This was one of the most difficult things Yolanda had ever done. It was painful (extremely uncomfortable), and Yolanda feared that Beverly would hate her. She was right.

Beverly was furious with her mother. She soon found another job, but it did not pay nearly as well, and she did not like it as much. She and Sal had to sell their house because they could not make the payments on Sal's salary alone.

After several months of furious anger at her mother, Beverly began to realize that *she* had "blown it" and took full responsibility for her actions. She and Sal moved into an apartment that they could afford. Their marriage improved, and Beverly started to save money to repay her mother. Although she had felt resentful at first, she realized that she was proud of herself when the money was paid back in full. It felt good to learn that she could stand on her own two feet.

As more time passed, Beverly slowly realized she was also proud of her mother for doing what was right in a kind and firm manner. After all, she could have heaped on blame, shame, and even jail. (Avoiding those lectures had been very difficult for Yolanda.) Instead of going for the comfort of the moment (and sometimes anger and revenge feel very comfortable), her mother had helped them both become better people through the painful but essential process of kind and firm weaning.

It is difficult to accept that doing the wisest, best thing for our children may not make us *feel* wonderful. Life would undoubtedly be simpler if parents could navigate by following their emotions. But doing so— and who among us hasn't given in to emotion at least once or twice?—inevitably leads us into dangerous waters. Wise and truly loving parents learn to guide their children's course by using their hearts *and* their heads. If you believe that your children may one day need to make it on their own, without your constant supervision and service, and if you want them to experience the pride that comes from accomplishing something in life, you will understand that weaning them is not only necessary but the most loving thing you can do.

CHAPTER 9

Character Education at Home

Character is the word that sums up what is missing from most children who are loved too much. Instead of developing character, these children all too often develop such "characteristics" as self-centeredness, selfishness, and rebelliousness; they often become demanding, dissatisfied, weak, and otherwise unattractive and ineffective. All parents want their children to develop good character; they recognize its importance to children's future happiness and success. But loving too much does not build character in children. Instead, character often grows from the experiences we enjoy the least—and from what we learn from and decide about those experiences.

Some famous people—people of great character themselves—have spoken up on the issue of character and what "grows" it. Here is a sampling of their wisdom:

The ultimate measure of a man is not where he stands in moments of comfort, but where he stands at times of challenge and controversy.
—*Martin Luther King Jr.*

(How can children develop character if they are protected from challenge and controversy instead of being encouraged to develop skills to deal with those challenges?)

Our character is what we do when we think no one is looking.
—*H. Jackson Browne*

(Excessive control, punishment, or pampering often create an "external locus of control" in children. That is, children look outside themselves to find reasons and rewards for their actions. People with character usually have an *internal* locus of control—they choose an action because they know it is the right thing to do.)

Nearly all men can stand adversity, but if you want to test a man's character, give him power.
—*Abraham Lincoln*

(Will your children use their personal power for personal gain or to make a contribution to the world? To which end are they being trained?)

Character cannot be developed in ease and quiet. Only through experiences of trial and suffering can the soul be strengthened, ambition inspired, and success achieved.
—*Helen Keller*

(Helen Keller's parents were raising a spoiled brat until Annie Sullivan came into her life and loved her enough to insist that she learn to be capable in spite of her physical challenges.)

How Do Children Develop Character?

Parents who love "too much" usually are doing what is easy (or what "feels good") instead of what is right. They are following their emotions instead of using methods based on knowledge and understanding of long-term results. They don't think about what it takes to develop character, or they do not realize that character does not come from being pampered or controlled. They don't understand that character is learned and developed through the kinds of experiences that teach:

> People with character usually have an *internal* locus of control: they choose actions because they know it is the right thing to do.

- Respect for self and others
- Desire to contribute to the welfare of others and the community
- Honesty
- Integrity
- Hard work
- Self-discipline
- Accountability
- Gratitude
- Courage
- Resiliency

Children Are Not Born with Character

Children are born with temperaments and definite personality traits, but they are not born with character. As stated earlier, character must be taught and learned experientially. Lectures about being respectful, fair, responsible, and helpful just don't work. Lectures only "teach" defensiveness, avoidance, and possibly low self-esteem. The only experiences children are likely to have while listening to lectures are feelings of inadequacy, rebelliousness, or just plain boredom. In fact, many children learn to tune out lecturing adults after about ten words!

Education comes from the Latin word *educare*, which means "to draw forth." Adults can "draw forth" by creating opportunities for children to learn from their own experience as they find out for themselves how it feels to focus on solutions or to give service to others. Too often, parents try to teach by stuffing *in* through lectures and then wonder why it goes *in* and *out*.

Four Basic Needs: The Foundation for Character Education at Home

Throughout this book, we refer to the four main ideas that lead to the development of good character. All of these needs are discussed throughout this book and are summarized here as the foundation to the development of character. What are these basic human needs? To become capable, competent, happy people who are able to make a contribution to those around them and enjoy life to the fullest, children (and all the rest of us as well) need

1. A sense of belonging and significance
2. Perceptions of capability
3. Personal power and autonomy
4. Social and life skills used for contribution to society as well as for personal happiness

A Sense of Belonging and Significance

Ask a group of parents what they believe to be most important in raising healthy, happy children, and many will give you a simple answer: love. But love by itself is not enough, as we are beginning to see; in fact, most parenting mistakes are made in the name of love. As we keep pointing out in this book, there are many definitions of love, and some of those definitions don't help children feel belonging and significance or learn the attitudes and skills they will need to live successful, happy lives.

Alfred Adler taught about our need as human beings to belong, to have a place in the world that is ours alone, a place where we can be accepted and where we can believe in our own value and significance. If we were to condense into a few words all the complicated beliefs and attitudes that children need to grow into competent, confident adults, those words would be "a sense of belonging and significance."

All of us want to belong somewhere, to be accepted for who and what we are, and to be loved unconditionally. For children, the need to belong is even more overwhelming. Each child needs to know that there is a place in his family just for him, where he fits and is accepted unconditionally. As children grow, their peers often provide that sense of belonging. (If you doubt it, spend an hour or two in the halls of any middle school. Why do you suppose it matters to children what logo adorns their clothing, which athletic shoe they wear, or how their hair is styled?) The more self-confidence and skills they have, the less likely they are to be overly influenced by "the crowd."

Children who don't believe they belong become discouraged, and discouraged children often misbehave. Have you ever noticed how much of your children's misbehavior seems to shout, "Notice me! Involve me! Pay attention to my feelings! Don't boss me around! Help me succeed!"? Misbehavior is a sort of "code" for a child's unspoken need to belong.

Everyone is concerned about the violence that has taken place in our schools over the past few years. These horrifying incidents have provided a wake-up call for the great need to make serious changes in our homes and schools. Kids who are killing other kids and adults did not feel belonging and significance. When kids do not feel belonging and significance, they usually choose one of four mistaken goals of behavior to compensate. They seek undue attention, misguided power, or revenge, or they withdraw into assumed inadequacy. Students who engage in violence have chosen the most terrible kind of revenge.

Even the FBI has joined the search to find out what is at the root of the violence in schools today. They have

PEANUTS © UFS. Reprinted by Permission.

interviewed the young men who have committed these crimes and found that the core problem was a lack of a sense of belonging. Not only did these young men believe that they didn't belong (that no one cared), they also said that they were teased. They felt—and eventually began to act—like outcasts and aliens among their peers, which fueled the flames that led to revenge. You may wonder what this example has to do with loving too much, since these children felt very *un*loved. This extreme example shows the power of the basic need to belong.

The problem with loving too much is that too many parents try to help their children feel a sense of belonging and significance in ways that create just the opposite feeling. Children don't feel a sense of belonging and significance when parents coddle or control. Instead these children usually develop the belief, "I belong only when you do things for me, or give me constant attention, or rescue me, or order me around." Rather than helping children develop confidence in their own abilities and a sense of belonging that comes from within, loving too much fosters dependence on others.

There are many ways of creating a sense of belonging for children; we have already mentioned family meetings, which are expanded on later in this chapter, and will discover more tools in the chapters ahead. For the moment, consider that the greater your child's sense of belonging and significance, the less often she will need to resort to misbehavior and the more confidence and self-discipline she will have. Helping children develop a healthy sense of belonging and significance is the cornerstone of healthy love.

Perceptions of Capability

How can children develop the belief that they are capable if they are not allowed to experience their capability? Many parents and teachers are robbing their children of opportunities to develop this important belief by doing too much for them and by trying to grant their every desire. However, there is a huge difference between what children need and what they want. Children want special service. But giving special service robs them of the opportunity to learn they are capable of helping themselves. Children want every toy they see. But giving them every toy they see teaches them materialism and robs them of the ability to learn that they can handle disappointment or that they can work for what they want. Simply put, the more parents do *for* children, the less capable and motivated those children seem to feel. Merely *telling* children that they are capable doesn't work. Words alone are not powerful enough to build a sense of capability and competence in children. That perception can only come from experience.

Capability and self-esteem. Let's return for a moment to the subject of school violence. Many experts have focused on self-esteem—how children perceive their own worth and capability—as a cause of aggression. But is it *low* self-esteem that creates problems or self-esteem that is too *high?* In 1998, the American Psychological Association sponsored a study that unearthed an interesting fact. The young people most prone to aggression were those who had an excessively strong need to believe in their own superiority and specialness (a trait sometimes called *narcissism*). When others didn't find these youngsters special or failed to praise them sufficiently, they were likely to see anger or violence as an appropriate reaction.

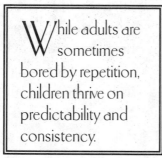

While adults are sometimes bored by repetition, children thrive on predictability and consistency.

Think for a moment about the self-esteem programs promoted in so many of our schools—with, it should be added, the best intentions in the world. Posters in classrooms proclaim, "I am lovable and capable." Or "I am special. When I like myself, others will like me too." But what happens if they don't? What if a child buys into this self-esteem message, only to find that the words were not enough?

As we have already seen, true self-esteem grows from perceptions of capability, from the skills and attitudes that allow children to learn that they are competent people. We have already discussed why it is important for children to dress themselves and that parents too often choose expedience and appearances instead of helping their children develop perceptions of capability by teaching skills—and expecting occasional mistakes along the way.

Capability and mistakes. Many parents (and many other adults) regard mistakes as sins, experiences that are fatal if not eliminated. The typical response of many parents to their children's inevitable mistakes is to punish, rescue, or attempt to prevent mistakes from happening at all. Others believe they are letting their children "get away with something" if they don't at least impose a consequence. Perhaps the best way to respond to a mistake (and who hasn't made one or two in the process of growing up or learning a new skill?) is to help children clean up the mess, whatever it is, and then learn how not to make that particular mess again. Punishing mistakes or rescuing children from ever making them will not help children develop perceptions of capability. Instead, teach your children that mistakes are actually wonderful opportunities to learn.

Mark Twain once said, "Good judgment comes from experience. Experience comes from bad judgment."

Children sometimes do choose to learn "the hard way." (Remember, *education* means "to draw forth," not to stuff in.)

Exploring consequences to help children develop perceptions of capability. Instead of *imposing* a consequence (which is usually an ineffective way to disguise punishment), parents can help children explore for themselves the consequences of their choices. This can be done through the respectful use of "what" and "how" questions:

What happened?
What were you trying to accomplish?
How do you feel about what happened?
What did you learn from this experience?
How could you use what you learned in the future?
What ideas do you have to solve this problem now?

Remember, the point is to help children explore the consequences of their actions. This purpose is voided if you use a sarcastic tone of voice or if you are trying to get them to think what you think. They will know the difference. It is interesting that if you are sincerely curious in your questioning, your children often will end up thinking what you think. When children feel truly listened to and can see that you really do care what they think, they have the opportunity to *explore* the consequences of their choices by thinking it through, which also helps them become acquainted with positive uses for their personal power.

Personal Power and Autonomy

Parents may not like it, but the fact remains that children *do* have personal power and they will use it. The only question is *how* will they use that power? Will they use it in constructive or destructive ways? Will they engage in power struggles, or will they use their power for social interest, cooperation, and contribution?

> The young people most prone to aggression were those who had an excessively strong need to believe in their own superiority and specialness.

Parents who love in permissive ways teach children to use their personal power to manipulate. Parents who love in controlling ways teach their children to use their personal power for rebellion or, worse, compliance. (Overly compliant children run the risk of becoming "people pleasers," putting them at the mercy of those who are stronger or louder than they are.)

Are you providing enough opportunities in your home for your children to use their power in constructive ways? Are you giving your children choices? (Limited choices for young children, and broader choices as they grow older.) Are you having family meetings at which children are respectfully involved in brainstorming for solutions and in creating limits and routines? Do you provide training in problem solving and then have faith in your children to solve their own problems (or to learn from the results of their occasional failures)? Are you providing opportunities for them to use their power to help others? Are you teaching them decision-making and problem-solving skills by involving them and providing them with opportunities to practice these skills? One of the best ways to address this need (as well as the other basic needs) is to use effective family meetings. (Family meetings are discussed in detail later in this chapter.)

Social and Life Skills Used for Contribution to Society as Well as for Personal Happiness

Providing opportunities for children to learn social and life skills is one of the best ways to help them develop character. Dr. Thomas J. Stanley made some very interesting discoveries when interviewing millionaires for his book *The Millionaire Mind* (McMeel, 2000). We certainly are not saying that acquiring lots of money is necessary to be a successful person. In fact, most of the millionaires interviewed by Stanley were also happy, contributing members of society who did not spend their considerable wealth in the flashy and selfish ways you might expect. (Money is neutral; it can be used in both positive and negative ways.) Still, it is interesting to examine the background and choices of people who have achieved a high level of the quality that society labels "success."

Interestingly enough, high academic grades were not the most important factor in the millionaires' achievements. In fact, most of the people interviewed were not scholars. Most had been told they were not intellectually gifted and that they were not smart enough to succeed (p. 14). What they *did* learn (but not from textbooks) was tenacity, the ability to get along with people, self-discipline, and discernment (p. 15). The five factors most often mentioned by millionaires as being very important in explaining their economic success are

1. Integrity—being honest with all people
2. Discipline—applying self-control
3. Social skills—getting along with people
4. Having a supportive partner
5. Hard work—more than most people are willing to do (p. 11)

Obviously, school is not unimportant. But most parents spend a tremendous amount of time hounding their children about doing their homework and getting good grades but very little time providing opportunities for their children to develop integrity, self-discipline, and social skills or to work hard to earn whatever they get. Most of the millionaires in Stanley's survey went to school and applied self-discipline to work hard. But that is the difference—*self*-discipline and hard work rather than too much control or rescuing from parents.

Parents can help their children develop self-discipline by involving them in the creation of plans and routines that work for the child, and then using "what" and "how" questions to help them explore the consequences when they make mistakes. Sometimes the best lesson children can experience is failure. What a great opportunity for them to explore what happened, what caused it to happen, how they feel about it, and what they want to do about it. (In fact, children are astonishingly resilient and are well equipped to learn from failure; it's their parents who struggle with the concept!)

Social skills—getting along with others—appears third on Stanley's list. Social skills, which involve compassion, respect, empathy, communication, and old-fashioned good manners, are among the most important skills children can learn, especially when those skills are used to contribute to society. What good are all the academic skills in the world, if those skills are used in selfish or hurtful ways? What good is self-discipline and hard work, if it is used only in self-serving ways? Everyone benefits when children learn to give as well as to receive.

USA Today's **All USA High School Academic Teams.** The May 11, 2000, edition of *USA Today* introduced that newspaper's "All USA High School Academic Teams." Each one of these amazing teens had initiated a project designed to make contributions to society. Following is a list of some of their projects:

- Tutor to disadvantaged children
- Tutor at public housing projects
- Upward Bound tutor
- Musical performer in nursing and convalescent homes
- Creator of a music stimulation program for Alzheimer's patients
- Founder of "Read and Lead Foundation," a literacy mentoring program that expanded internationally
- Founder of America Online tutoring club

- Habitat for Humanity volunteer
- Hospital volunteer

Family Meetings

An important part of family meetings could be to help children find projects in which they can make a contribution to others. Because character is taught, not caught, there are many other activities you can provide during family meetings to provide opportunities

> Children are astonishingly resilient and are well-equipped to learn from failure; it's their parents who struggle with the concept!

for the development of character—if you are thinking about the long-range effects of your parenting decisions and are aware that children are looking to you to teach it to them (whether they know it or not).

As we have learned, children develop character when their four basic emotional needs are met. One of the simplest, yet most powerful, ways to meet all of a child's basic needs is to hold family meetings. Family meetings provide a powerful format for helping children develop character through respectful involvement and meaningful contribution. During family meetings, children feel belonging and significance because their thoughts and ideas are listened to, taken seriously, and validated. Family meetings also help children to feel capable, use their personal power in useful ways, develop perceptions of capability, and learn important social and life skills.

It is extremely important to have family meetings on a weekly basis at a specified time. It is so easy for the demands of our busy lifestyles to intrude on our family time. Children need to know that they are as important as any business or social meeting their parents may schedule.

Family meetings help children feel capable, use their personal power in useful ways, develop perceptions of capability, and learn important social and life skills.

Family meetings should begin with compliments and appreciations and then proceed to brainstorming for solutions to any problems that may have been put on the family meeting agenda during the week. They should end by planning for family fun times. Many families do not spend enough time together doing fun things. They have good intentions; but they don't take the time to plan and schedule events on a calendar—and then life gets in the way. To make sure you have time together as a family, you might want to use the Family Meeting Fun Time Planning Activity.

During family meetings, children learn to communicate—they learn to speak and to listen. They learn to respect differences. They learn brainstorming and problem-solving skills. They learn to help each other and to contribute to each other.

The magic key is involvement. When children are respectfully involved in effective family meetings, they take ownership. They have enthusiasm and motivation to follow rules and guidelines they helped create. During

Family Meeting Fun Time Planning Activity

1. Use a Fun Things to Do sheet (see sample) for a brainstorming session with the whole family. Under the Together as a Family column, list your ideas for both free things to do and things that cost money.

2. Make copies of this sheet, and give copies to all family members so they can continue to list things they think of during the week, not only for the whole family but also for things to do alone (listed under the Alone column).

3. During family meetings, let the family choose from the list something from the Together as a Family column. Be sure to set a date for this activity. Then have each person share what he or she would like to schedule as something to do alone. (Believe it or not, children are quite capable of entertaining themselves, when they are invited to do so and helped to learn how. The alternative is to appoint yourself chief social director of your family and hear a constant litany of "I'm bored!")

Fun Things to Do

Together as a Family		Husband and Wife		Alone	
Free	For $	Free	For $	Free	For $

this process, they have many opportunities to develop the beliefs that they belong and are significant, that they are capable, that they can use their power and autonomy in constructive ways, and that they can develop the social skills and life skills and character that lead them to become happy, contributing members of society.

Creating Routine Charts

One of the best ways to demonstrate healthy love is to teach children to contribute and cooperate by respectfully involving them (yes, we are saying it again) in the creation of routines. Why, you may ask, are routines important? If you've ever caught yourself complaining about how difficult it is to get out the door in the morning, or about the hassles involved in getting your children to bed at a decent time (consider for a moment the endless nagging and reminding so often a part of these processes), routines may be just what you're looking for.

While adults are sometimes bored by repetition, children thrive on predictability and consistency. Routines—organized, repeated ways of doing everyday tasks—have a charming way of becoming the "boss"; all a parent needs to do is ask the child, "What's next in our routine chart?" Family meetings are a great time to create bedtime routines, morning routines, mealtime routines, and homework routines. Keep in mind that children are more willing to follow routines when they have been respectfully involved in creating them— which also gives them the opportunity to learn that they are capable.

Family Meeting Gratitude Activity

1. At the end of each family meeting, pass out a blank Gratitude Page. Encourage family members to put the page in a place where they can access it easily and write down the things for which they are grateful.

2. Allow time during family meals for people to share the things for which they are grateful.

3. During each family meeting, collect the Gratitude Pages, and place them in a folder. Some families enjoy reading their Gratitude Pages once a year as part of a Thanksgiving ritual.

The Role of Gratitude

Good character requires an attitude of gratitude, which does not come naturally. Gratitude must be learned and is one of the traits that parents can model effectively for their children. Regular practice and sharing will help all of you develop an attitude of gratitude. Some families include sharing two or three things that they are grateful for as part of their bedtime routine. Try using the Family Meeting Gratitude Activity at one of your next family meetings.

Family Mottoes

Your family can create a sense of belonging and closeness—and have a great time—by creating family mottoes.

All families have mottoes, although most are unwritten and unacknowledged. Mottoes can be positive and encouraging, or negative and discouraging. One woman in a workshop laughed and told the group that the motto in the family she grew up in was "Knock yourself out—and it still won't be good enough unless it's perfect." A recovering perfectionist in her 40s, this woman shared that her family's motto (and the decisions she and her siblings made about themselves as a result) was more powerful precisely because it remained unspoken.

> All families have mottoes, although most are unwritten and unacknowledged.

What was the motto in the family you grew up in? What do you suppose the motto is in the family you have created? What beliefs do you want your children to adopt? You might want to choose a different motto every month and give each motto meaning through the suggested activities. Several examples of encouraging family mottoes are included here; you may want to use some of these and/or create your own:

Sample Mottoes
1. One for all and all for one.
2. We love and support each other.
3. Anything worth doing is worth doing for the fun of it.
4. If it helps just one person, it is worth doing.
5. Mistakes are wonderful opportunities to learn.
6. We are good finders.

Family Meeting Motto Activity

1. Have the whole family choose a motto for the month.

2. Week 1: Give each family member a sheet of paper with a fancy heading that says, "Our Family Motto." (Invite your children to provide the artwork.) Ask each family member to think about the motto during the week and to write down his or her thoughts about what it means to them. (Set up special times to take dictation from children who are too young to write.)

3. Week 2: Plan time during the family meeting for each person to share what he or she wrote. Place all these sheets in a family binder. Pass out another motto sheet and invite everyone to find some time during the week to draw a picture that represents what the motto means to him or her. You might want to plan a special time when everyone does this together.

4. Week 3: Plan time during the family meeting for each person to share his or her picture and talk about it. Place the pictures on the refrigerator or some other place where everyone can enjoy them. Ask family members to notice how they apply the family motto in action during the following week.

5. Week 4: Plan time during the family meeting for each person to share an example of how they used the family motto in action. Invite family members to be thinking about another motto for the next month.

6. Week 1 of the Next Month: Put all the drawings of the previous month's motto in the family binder. Choose another motto, and repeat the process.

7. We are problem solvers.
8. We look for solutions rather than blame.
9. We have an attitude of gratitude.
10. We count our blessings every day.

Meal Planning as a Character Builder

Have you ever grumbled about the drudgery of planning meals, shopping for them, cooking them, and cleaning up afterward? Did you know meals provide a terrific opportunity to teach the character traits of cooperation and contribution? Even small children can take a turn cooking a simple meal such as soup and toasted cheese sandwiches, a vegetable, lettuce salad, and Jell-O. You might want to try the Family Meal Planning Activity.

> You can help your children become good finders and create a positive atmosphere in your family when everyone learns to look for the good in each other and verbalize positive comments.

Good Finding

In his book *In Search of Excellence* (Warner, 1988), Tom Peters says that successful people are "good finders." You can help your children become good finders and create a positive atmosphere in your family when everyone learns to look for the good in one another and verbalize positive comments. But please, don't expect

Family Meeting Meal Planning Activity

1. During the family meeting, use a Family Meal Planning Page (see sample) to get every family member involved in planning the meals for a week.

2. Bring magazines that contain recipes to the family meeting. Let children (and parents) choose new recipes they might want to try. (It can be fun to make a family cookbook by cutting out the recipes and pictures and putting them in a binder. Family members might first want to rate the recipes for taste and save only the ones that receive a high rating.)

3. Use 3-by-5 cards for recipes. On the back of the recipe, write all the ingredients needed from the store. (Save these cards in a special card index box so they can be used over and over.)

4. On shopping day, take the whole family to the grocery store. Children who are old enough can take a basket and find all the ingredients listed on the back of one or two recipe cards. Depending on how many children you have, each child may take one card or more than one. You can check to see if you also need any of the staple items such as sugar, salt, and flour that may be listed on the back of the cards, and make sure only one person picks up these items. Younger children can help an older sibling or parent find the ingredients from other recipe cards.

Family Meal Planning Page

	Cook	Main Dish	Vegetable	Salad	Dessert
Mon.					
Tues.					
Etc.					

Family Meeting Compliments Activity

1. Place blank compliment sheets on the refrigerator (or another spot) where everyone can write down compliments for others each day. (Young children can dictate their compliments to older members of the family.)

2. When you see someone who deserves a compliment, write it down. If a child observes something someone else did, ask "Would you like to write that on our compliment sheet?" Once children develop the habit of noticing compliments, they won't need reminders.

3. At the beginning of each family meeting, family members can read their compliments.

4. Ask for any verbal compliments that were not written down.

5. Make sure every family member receives at least one compliment.

6. Place this compliment sheet in a folder, and place another blank sheet on the refrigerator to be filled out during the week. Reading the compliments (saved in a folder) many years later can be as much fun as looking at old picture albums.

perfection! Some sibling squabbling is normal. However, when children (and parents) learn to give and receive compliments, negative tension in the family is reduced considerably.

Gemeinschaftsgefühl

Alfred Adler coined the word *Gemeinschaftsgefühl* in writing about the qualities healthy people possess. As with many German words and phrases, there is no precise translation into English, but the phrase that Adlerians have settled for is "social interest." Still, *Gemeinschaftsgefühl* means so much more than those two words can convey. It means a feeling of community, a concern for one's fellow people, for the environment, and everything that is required for quality of life and relationships. It also implies the need for actions necessary to live a charactered life for oneself and for humanity. Adler believed that healthy people had a learned desire to contribute to their community, other people, and the world around them. Social interest is the polar opposite of self-centeredness—one of the traits so frequently bemoaned in today's young people.

If our children develop the character required for *Gemeinschaftsgefühl,* just think what our families, neighborhoods, schools, communities, and world could become. It will be a challenge; but it is a challenge all parents must dare to accept.

CHAPTER 10

Healthy Loving

More of What Children
Really Need

Marissa and her mother are taking a plane trip from their home in Denver to San Francisco, where Marissa's grandparents live. Mom has brought a book and settles down to read; once the excitement of the take-off is past, Marissa begins looking for something to do. Her mother has brought a small bag of toys, but Marissa, who is five, is finished with those toys in about fifteen minutes. She sits grumpily in her seat, kicking the seat in front of her and rhythmically dropping and picking up the tray table. After a dirty look from the woman in the seat ahead of her, Marissa's mother tells her, "Stop that, Marissa," without looking up from her book.

Now Marissa turns her attention to the man sitting next to her. A well-dressed businessman, he is working on a complicated spreadsheet on his laptop computer. Marissa reaches over with an impish grin and taps one of the keys. The man smiles and says kindly, "Computers are fun, aren't they? But I'm working on something important right now. Please don't touch my computer." Marissa stops grinning and hits another key, at which point her mother grabs Marissa's arm, yanks it back, and says, "Marissa, leave the man alone!"

Marissa sulks but is distracted by the approach of the beverage cart. She gets a soda from the attendant, and when the woman gives her a shiny bag of pretzels, Marissa says, "I want *two*." Then she spills her soda. Mom tries to wipe off the papers of the man sitting next to Marissa, switches places with her wailing daughter, and sinks down into her seat as far as she can. San Francisco is still more than two hours away.

By now, you're probably wondering what is wrong with Marissa's mother. But as anyone who has flown on an airplane, shopped at the mall, or eaten at a fast-food restaurant lately can tell you, children like Marissa are everywhere. It might be easy to decide that Marissa needs a good spanking, or a stern lecture, or a time-out. But what is it that Marissa—and all children—*really* need?

The Building Blocks of Healthy Love

Many children seem to require endless attention and special service from the adults around them. They are easily bored and unable to entertain themselves for more than a few moments, or they've developed the art of manipulation and whining to a fine degree. As they grow older, their behavior usually escalates and can become truly dangerous, to themselves and others. But the problem goes far deeper than just managing behavior. Too many parents fail to understand what is required to teach children cooperation, self-discipline, responsibility, and respect. These qualities rarely develop on their own; they must be conscientiously nurtured (and it helps if adults have them first!)

There are a number of concepts to consider in deciding how to love our children in healthy ways. We have already discussed many of the things children *really* need, such as a sense of belonging and significance, personal power, and social and life skills. They also need

- The development of mutual respect and dignity
- An opportunity to develop strength in The Significant Seven
- Social interest
- An ability to recognize and manage feelings

The Development of Mutual Respect and Dignity

Most adults, from teachers to grandparents to Scout leaders, frequently comment on the astonishing lack of respect young people seem to have for others these days. It is important to note that a great many young people are respectful, polite, and appreciative, but it is also true that indeed many are not. Respect—for others and for oneself—is essential to healthy relationships. How do children learn it?

One father commented recently in an Internet parenting chat room that he had no patience for all these newfangled parenting ideas. "My kid will respect me when he fears me," he said, "and I know how to make him fear me." But are fear and respect the same? And are they part of love? We believe one of the key ingredients of love is respect. However, it seems that, as with love, respect also has too many definitions, most of which do not fit the kind of respect that is loving and empowering to children.

Think for a moment of someone you respect. What qualities does that person have? Why do you respect him or her? Would you like your children to feel that way about you? Do you feel that way about your children?

> Loving too much fosters dependence on others.

The fact is that children learn respect, like so many other character qualities, when they see it in action. Respect means valuing people for their innate worth and uniqueness, despite the fact that their feelings and ideas may be different from your own. Mutual respect means valuing yourself as well as others and knowing that although you can't control others, you can control yourself. For example, it doesn't help to say to a child who has just talked back, "You are not allowed to talk to me like that." This is silly, because the child just did it. Nor does it help to punish. That simply takes the behavior underground. Surely you have heard a child mutter something under her breath, and you know it is disrespectful. However, when you demand, "What did you say?" the child replies, "Nothing."

It is more effective, respectful, and self-loving to say, "I will not stand here while you are talking to me in disrespectful ways. We can talk later when we both can be respectful." Then leave. Follow up by putting the problem on a family meeting agenda (or on a list for some one-on-one time) for problem solving.

Children learn respect when parents demonstrate it, when they respect themselves enough to decide what they will do, and when parents respect one another, other adults, and, yes, their children. Children can also learn

> Mutual respect means valuing yourself as well as others and knowing that although you can't control others, you can control yourself.

disrespect when they witness yelling, bigotry, dishonesty, or the everyday rudeness so commonplace in our society today.

We often quote Alfred Adler because he was a pioneer in the concept of respect for all people. His definition of respect includes equality, which does not mean "the same." Equality means that all people—even young people—have equal worth, despite their differences. Adler believed that all people, including children, should be treated with dignity and respect. Incidentally, respecting children does not mean giving them adult rights and privileges. It means choosing not to use shame or humiliation to shape their behavior, practicing discipline skills that teach rather than punish, and accepting that although children may not have equal rights with adults, they do have equal worth as human beings. It also means that parents must treat themselves (and each other) with respect. When parents are disrespectful of each other or put their children's needs ahead of everyone else's (including their own), children may be learning in subtle ways to disregard the rights and feelings of others. In other words, children are not the only members of the family who deserve a sense of belonging and significance: moms and dads do, too! The practice of respect is an essential part of healthy love.

Mutual respect and dignity are often related to feelings of belonging and significance—or lack thereof. Marissa, our little friend from the airplane, had decided somewhere along the way that she belonged only when she was receiving lots of attention from adults. When no one was paying attention, she found many effective ways to *get* attention. The tragedy of misbehavior is that it *works;* parents do pay attention to misbehaving children in the wrong ways, often unintentionally reinforcing the misbehavior.

An Opportunity to Develop Strength in the Significant Seven

In *Raising Self-Reliant Children in a Self-Indulgent World* (Prima, 2000), H. Stephen Glenn and Jane Nelsen outlined three perceptions and four skills they called the "Significant Seven" (see page 210), attributes that equip children as well as adults to lead successful, effective lives.

Obviously, a great many adults lack these attributes, and loving too much doesn't nurture these resources. So, how do children acquire them?

One of the most insidious symptoms of loving too much is the tendency of so many parents to do *everything* for their children. On the surface, it certainly looks

The Significant Seven: Seven Resources of
Highly Resilient and Capable People

1. **Strong perceptions of personal capabilities:** "I am capable of facing problems and challenges and gaining strength and wisdom through experience."

2. **Strong perceptions of significance:** "My life has meaning and purpose, and I contribute in unique and meaningful ways."

3. **Strong perceptions of personal influence over life:** "I can influence what I do in life and am accountable for my actions and choices."

4. **Strong intrapersonal skills:** the ability to manage personal emotions through self-assessment, self-control, and self-discipline

5. **Strong interpersonal skills:** the ability to communicate, cooperate, negotiate, share, empathize, listen, and work effectively with people

6. **Strong systemic skills:** the ability to respond to the limits and consequences of everyday life with responsibility, adaptability, flexibility, and integrity

7. **Strong judgmental skills:** the ability to make decisions based on moral and ethical principles, wisdom, and understanding

loving: children want for nothing, are well taken care of, are not burdened by onerous chores and responsibilities, and have everything they want at their fingertips. But what are they learning? The inherent danger in doing everything *for* your children is that they may decide they are not capable of doing it for themselves.

One mother recently told her parenting group that her son could never seem to remember to take his lunch, his jacket, and his homework to school. "What do you do about that?" the group's facilitator asked. "I drop his stuff at the school each morning," the mother answered. "I don't want him to be cold or hungry or to get bad grades from not turning in his work." As long as this boy's mom is willing to ride to his rescue each day, he has no need to develop organizational skills, self-discipline, or

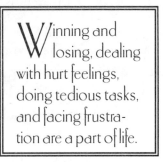

Winning and losing, dealing with hurt feelings, doing tedious tasks, and facing frustration are a part of life.

self-control. This mother might be surprised at how quickly her child would learn if he were allowed to experience cold, hunger, or a low grade. Children do not drop dead from a missed meal, children who don't wear jackets do not come down with pneumonia, and as we have already said, failure can be a valuable life experience when it is accepted as simply another learning opportunity.

It is important to note that we don't advocate punishing children by making them miss meals. Nor is it ever acceptable to neglect children. However, it can be very effective and empowering to help a children explore the consequences of their choices by empathetically asking, "What do you think caused that to happen, and what ideas do you have to solve the problem?"

One of the most encouraging things any parent can do is to *teach*, to give children opportunities to learn the skills they will need to be successful people. The problem is that teaching takes time and patience: many parents find it easier—"just for now"—to do things *for* children or to punish them for their mistakes. When children learn that hassling and whining will make parents give in and do the work themselves or that punishment is a small price to pay for irresponsibility, the prospects are bleak indeed.

Mark, a single father, dreaded laundry day. His daughter's clothes were rarely in the basket, and he found himself hunting in the closet and under her bed for missing articles. Gwen, ten, played a lot of sports and left her sweaty socks in damp wads; Mark detested turning them right side out. Mark believed he had tried everything: he'd lectured, threatened, and made huge heaps of Gwen's dirty clothes on her bedroom floor. Nothing fazed Gwen; she went right on leaving her clothes and wadded socks wherever she pleased. Eventually, Mark would gather everything up and wash it.

Mark was groaning about Gwen's habits to a friend one evening. "Why do you keep picking up after her?" his friend asked. Mark discovered that he didn't have a good answer. Gwen's behavior was certainly working well for her! It occurred to Mark that if his daughter was going to live on her own someday, she might need to know how to deal with her laundry.

That weekend, Mark sat down with his daughter and had a calm, friendly talk. "You know, Gwen, I get frustrated looking for your things and peeling your socks apart. From now on," he said kindly, "I'm only going to wash what's in the laundry basket, and if you put your socks in there in wads, that's how I'll wash them. Whatever doesn't get washed will be your responsibility. I'll show you how to run the washer and dryer."

Gwen looked at her dad and rolled her eyes. "Whatever," she said with a shrug.

Mark stuck to his guns, and, as he had anticipated, trouble showed up right on schedule when Gwen stalked into his room on a Monday morning. "Where's my Abercrombie sweatshirt, Dad?" she said. "I want to wear it!"

"I don't know," Mark said. "Was it in the laundry basket?"

"I don't know," Gwen howled. " I don't know how to do this stuff. You've always done it all!" She went back to her room, where she discovered the missing sweatshirt behind her desk.

"Looks like you'll either have to wear it the way it is or wash it tonight," Mark said sympathetically—and left the room to finish getting dressed. He heard Gwen muttering to herself in her room but resisted the urge to rescue her or

> The inherent danger in doing everything *for* your children is that they may decide they are not capable of doing it for themselves.

solve the problem for her. Sure enough, that evening Gwen sat down at the counter while her dad fixed dinner.

"Sorry about this morning," Gwen said. "I sorta lost it. Could you show me again how to do the wash? I found my best jeans under the bed."

Mark smiled. "Sure. Come here and I'll show you how to cook pasta. You can tell me about your day. And after dinner we'll have another go at the washer and dryer."

As time passed, Mark discovered that although he and Gwen still battled occasionally over chores, teaching her skills and then having faith in her ability to work things out helped both of them: he was less grumpy, and Gwen began to take pride in her ability to master the everyday tasks of managing her life. The process required energy and patience from both of them, but the long-term results for Gwen promised to be worth the effort.

The Significant Seven: A foundation for healthy self-esteem. Self-esteem is a nebulous concept. Most people believe that once you have achieved "good self-esteem" you have it forever, but in truth, self-esteem is something that seems to come and go, depending on the circumstances and how each person interprets those circumstances. A more useful approach to nurturing healthy children is encouraging capability skills and the self-confidence to handle the ups and downs of life, rather than the "warm and fuzzy" self-esteem taught by most parents and teachers. Capability and self-confidence do not grow from trophies, praise, smiley faces, or overprotection. They come from what have been called "competency experiences": the challenges each person must face and master as he or she grows and learns. Children need to be taught real-life skills and given opportunities to practice them. They can both enjoy their successes and learn from their mistakes (an equally important source of capability skills and self-confidence).

Parents who love in healthy ways recognize that their children need the opportunity to learn skills, make mistakes, and survive them. They need to stretch and grow a bit, to learn that they are capable of acquiring new abilities and taking risks. And children need to learn the sound judgment that comes from facing problems, exploring solutions, and learning from the results. Parents will not always be there to smooth the way for children. Healthy love means equipping children to succeed in a challenging and difficult world.

Social Interest

As we noted in the discussion of respect, many young people today do care, contribute, and cooperate in homes and communities. However, there are also many who do not, whose primary interest in life is "What's in it for me?" Is it important to teach your children to care? And if so, how should you do it?

If you have the opportunity, sit and watch a group of young children at a preschool sometime. You may notice that they love to have "jobs," things that are their responsibility to do. Preschool teachers are usually taught the importance of providing opportunities for children to experience their capability and to develop social interest.

At home, many little ones beg to be allowed to help Mom and Dad, to run the vacuum or squirt cleaning solution on the bathtub. What happens to that desire to help out? As we have said before, when parents do too much for their children, children often develop the belief that love means getting others to do things for them, instead of learning to contribute.

Busy parents often tell children to "go play"—after all, teaching children skills is, as we have seen, time-consuming work, and they often fail to do jobs to our specifications. Unfortunately, adults sometimes fail to model generosity and social interest themselves. They are more interested in acquisition than giving; they have no time to volunteer; they sneer at those less fortunate, those "too lazy" to earn a living. Children watch, listen—and learn.

Opportunities to practice social interest and generosity can be found everywhere you look. Raising children to care about those around them not only prepares them for a valuable life, it may be one of the greatest legacies you can leave this world and it is an essential building block of healthy love.

The Ability to Recognize and Manage Feelings

In his book *Real Boys: Rescuing Our Sons from the Myths of Boyhood* (Random House, 1998), William Pollack describes how our culture has encouraged boys to disconnect from their feelings, to be strong and "fine" all of the time. This "disconnect" is, he believes, one of the reasons there are so many depressed, angry, and violent men in this world.

In truth, all of us, male and female, young and old, need to know how to manage our emotions. Emotions are the raw data of life. Reading our gut feelings and learning to use them in making decisions is part of developing sound judgment and problem-solving skills. Unfortunately, many people learn either to bury their emotions or to dump them on people around them. Neither approach is healthy.

Parents who love too much often are manipulated by their children's emotions. They want children to be "happy," and any sign that children are *not* happy is interpreted as a call to action. They rush in to entertain, soothe, or placate.

Self-soothing. Anxiety is a normal component of daily life. You get anxious when you are scared, when you don't get what you want, when you feel rejected, when you try something new, when you feel hurt, when you feel powerless. The list

> A more useful approach to nurturing healthy children is encouraging capability skills and the self-confidence to handle the ups and downs of life.

goes on and on—especially in our hectic modern world. The good news is that you are born with several coping (self-soothing) abilities and can learn other skills as well. The bad news is that many loving parents extinguish their children's self-soothing abilities by assuming responsibility for their children's feelings and stepping in too quickly to take over the job of soothing them. These parents fail to teach additional self-soothing skills because they are so busy "fixing" every problem a child encounters.

Self-soothing is the ability to monitor and handle emotions and to calm oneself down when anxious, upset, or stressed. Children are born with the ability to self-soothe.[1] How does self-soothing happen? When you feel anxious, self-soothing is the ability to come back to your center until you feel better. Sometimes it means learning to tolerate frustration or discomfort until it passes and knowing there are things you can do (such as take some time out) to ease the discomfort until it does pass. There are many degrees of anxiety; some anxiety requires more time for self-soothing than others.

Parents demonstrate healthy love when they have faith in their children to deal with their feelings. This does not mean refusing to offer comfort and support. However, sometimes the best support is to say, "I have faith in you to feel what you feel and to learn from it."

> The good news is that you are born with several coping (self-soothing) abilities and can learn other skills as well.

Another form of support requires teaching children the value of taking some "positive time-out" until they feel better. Children (and adults) can also learn that sometimes it helps to sit quietly (and perhaps to meditate for a while), go for a walk, read a book, or use some other distraction until disturbing feelings pass. Parents can teach their children to look for the "message" in their feelings. In other words, "What could this feeling teach me?" Parents might even ask their children whether they would

---

1. E. Z. Tronick and A. Gianino (*Zero to Three: Bulletin for the National Center for Clinical Infant Programs* 6, no. 3 (February 1986): 1–6) researched the ability to self-soothe in infants and discovered that they self-soothe several times in a minute. If you observe an infant, you will notice what Tronick and Gianino discovered. Infants will stare intently at a person or object for several seconds. Then they will look away to self-center before returning to stare at the same object or focusing on something else.

like company or some alone time. Alone time can be helpful to deal with upsetting feelings or just to develop the ability to do without constant stimulation.

Alone time.   Children need some alone time to maintain their inherent self-soothing ability. Parents who have taken responsibility for their children's feelings may believe that children need to be entertained all the time. There is nothing wrong with providing stimulation and entertainment for children; however, parents can learn to provide a balance between stimulation and alone time when they respect the innate ability to self-soothe. They might feel less guilty about allowing an infant to play alone with his toes (or even a rattle) instead of thinking he needs constant stimulation from adults. Parents also need to have more faith in their children to deal with their own feelings—even though it may take them a little time.

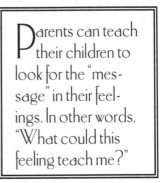

Parents can teach their children to look for the "message" in their feelings. In other words, "What could this feeling teach me?"

Let children have their feelings.   Another mistake made in the name of love is an attempt to control children's feelings, essentially telling children not to have feelings at all. "There's nothing to be afraid of," these parents insist. Or "Don't talk to me in that tone of voice, young lady!" Then there is the most prevalent of all: "Don't cry." After hearing, "Don't cry—I told you not to cry," many times, two-year-old Anthony would tremble and shake when he was hurt or afraid, but he would not cry. Children can learn to deny their feelings at a very young age.

Could it be that parents can't stand to watch their children experience pain because they have been taught to deny their own for so many years? Could it be that they think they are "protecting" their children from the judgments of others who might think their little boys are "sissies" if they cry, that they aren't learning to be "manly"? How many of you have heard this threat: "If you don't stop crying, I'll give you something to cry *about!*"

> Parents can learn to provide a balance between stimulation and alone time when they respect the innate ability to self-soothe.

Most parents feel acutely uncomfortable and anxious themselves when their children cry, whatever the reason. They react by attempting to protect their children from experiencing pain (sometimes because a child's crying stretches their own stressed-out nerves to the breaking point). But by stifling the expression of emotion, they create more pain. These well-meaning parents may create the opposite of what they intend. It is very painful for children to have their feelings discounted. What they need—and what nurtures their budding ability to self-soothe—is to have their feelings validated. "Wow," a parent might say, "that really hurt," or "You must have felt so scared!" Children usually feel encouraged when parents replace "Don't cry" with "It's okay to cry if you need to."

Most parents believe that a child's self-esteem is a fragile thing, easily damaged by competition, hurt feelings, or not having everything her friends have. Entire soccer leagues are built on the concept that no score will be kept—there will be no losers! Everyone gets a trophy and everyone wins—certainly an admirable goal. But ask any kid on either team, and he or she can tell you exactly what the score is. The truth is that winning and losing, dealing with hurt feelings, doing tedious tasks, and facing frustration are a part of life. Parents do their children no favors when they fail to teach the skills necessary for dealing with reality.

We have already mentioned the use of reflective and active listening, communication skills that can help parents (and children) identify and express feelings without being overwhelmed or manipulated by them. Parents who love in healthy ways learn how to listen to their children's feelings, identify the message those feelings are sending, and help children solve problems without rescuing, lecturing, or controlling. These children can learn to recognize their own emotions, learn from them, and communicate them in respectful ways, one of the most important parts of having strong relationships and peace of mind as an adult.

Giving Children What They Need

It may have occurred to you by now that giving your children healthy love—a sense of respect, life skills, social interest, and the ability to deal with emotions—is a lot of work. And it's true: loving children in healthy ways requires a great deal of patience, thought, and self-discipline. It means considering the long-range results of everyday actions. It means bearing the brunt of children's occasional disappointment and frustration. It means being strong enough and loving enough to do the hard work of raising healthy children.

> By stifling the expression of emotion, well-meaning parents may create the opposite of what they intend.

It is almost always easier to give children what they want (for the moment, anyway), but it is much more important, for our families and for the world we live in, to give children what they truly *need* to become healthy, happy, productive adults.

CHAPTER II

Where Change Begins
Understanding Yourself
as a Parent

It was Thursday morning, and that meant Emily was meeting her younger sister, Maggie, at their favorite coffeehouse. They had begun this ritual years ago and found that they both depended on this island of calm in their busy week, time to stay in touch with each other and share news of their own children and families. Today, though, Emily noticed immediately that Maggie looked tense and drawn.

"What's going on, Sis?" she asked with a sympathetic smile. Maggie took one look at her older sister's concerned face and dissolved into tears. "It's Amanda," she said. "What else?"

Emily handed Maggie a napkin and waited while her sister blew her nose and took a sip of her mocha. "I don't know what to do with the child," Maggie finally said. "I didn't think adolescence started until kids were

13 or 14, but Amanda is out of control and she's only 11. Last night she told me she was going to the mall with Jessie and Kim, her best friends, but Kim let it slip that they were meeting some eighth-grade boys. Amanda had put on makeup—I don't even know where she got it—and when I told her she was too young to go out with boys, she got right in my face and screamed at me. She called me a *bitch,* if you can believe that. And then I totally lost it. I still can't believe how angry I got. I told Jessie and Kim to leave, I shoved Amanda into her room, and I just yelled at her. She was yelling back, saying horrible things. I felt like slapping her. And in the middle of all this yelling, I remembered the fight I had with Mom when she wouldn't let me go to that party with Billy. Do you remember that?"

Emily nodded. "That was a pretty ugly scene, too."

Maggie began to weep again. "I always promised myself that if I ever had a daughter, I would never treat her like Mom treated me. We'd talk to each other and get along, and I would never yell at her. And now look at me. Amanda and I do nothing but fight. I love her, but I'm so worried—she's trying to grow up way too fast. And I don't know how to control her. What should I do?"

Many, many parents will feel empathy for Maggie. With the best intentions in the world, all of us make mistakes and say and do things with (and to) our children that we deeply regret. It's not hard to understand why impulsive, angry reactions to children's misbehavior cause problems, but, perhaps even more troubling, many loving parents have had the experience of thoughtfully choosing what they believe is best for their children, and then watching as those children misbehave, withdraw, make poor choices, reject their parents, get into trouble, or get deeply hurt. The risks young people face these days are so great; parents can only pray that the "trouble" their children get into isn't permanently damaging.

There are no perfect parents in this world of ours, and no perfect children. The good news is that perfection isn't necessary, and mistakes truly *are* opportunities to learn and grow. Long-term thinking, common sense, practical parenting tools, love, patience, and a little faith are the requirements for effective, healthy parenting. Yet many parents find that it is difficult to change, that even ideas that make sense are a challenge to implement. Many realize at some point along the way that they really don't know *why* they do what they do. And most of us have had the experience of "losing it" with our children and finding that all our worst traits come to the surface. What keeps parents from being able to express their love in healthy ways? What is it that makes positive change so difficult?

Parents Were Once Children: The Power of Experience

It has been said that those who cannot learn from history are doomed to repeat it. Relationships are rarely that simple or obvious, but it is true that parents often are reacting, consciously or unconsciously, to the experiences they had as children.

Take a moment to gaze out the window. You may see trees, buildings, or perhaps a busy street. Chances are that you don't notice the window frame or glass, yet they determine what you see. In the same way, the thoughts, feelings, and decisions you have accumulated throughout your own life shape the way you see yourself, your relationships, and your possibilities. Moreover, because you began making those decisions when you were very young, you may not be aware of how powerful they are. Maggie, for example, had made a conscious decision *not* to be the sort of parent her own mother was, yet she discovered that, in the midst of her concern for and anger at her daughter, she repeated her mother's hurtful, ineffective actions. Emily shares the same mother and many of the same genes and experiences, yet it is entirely possible that she has made different decisions—with different results—about raising her own children. Why?

> The good news is that perfection isn't necessary, and mistakes truly *are* opportunities to learn and grow.

Awareness—in this case, *self*-awareness—is the first step toward change. If you suspect that your love for your children has sometimes been expressed in ways that are not ultimately healthy or helpful, understanding yourself is the best way to understanding—and, perhaps, changing—your relationships.

How You Became the Person You Are

There is a long-standing debate about which is more important: heredity (your genes and the traits you physically inherit from your birth parents) or the environment (the conditions present in your family and physical setting). Many researchers and students of human behavior believe that each person's "personality" is actually the result of an intricate dance between these two factors.

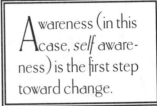

A wareness (in this case, *self* awareness) is the first step toward change.

Others, including Judith Rich Harris, author of *The Nurture Assumption: Why Children Turn Out the Way They Do* (Free Press, 1998) believe that parents have little or no influence on their children's personalities; genes and their peers are what determine a child's eventual personality.

Adlerian psychologists believe that there is a third factor that is at least as important as the other two: this factor is the unconscious decisions each person makes about what he or she must do to find belonging, safety, and significance. In other words, it isn't just what happens to you that is important: it's what you *decide* about what happens to you that makes a difference. What you decide creates the window (filter) and the framework of your perceptions. All future experiences are perceived and "colored" by the filter of your thought system.[1]

---

1. See *From Here to Serenity: Four Principles for Understanding Who You Really Are* (Prima, 2000) by Jane Nelsen, for more information on the thought system and how to see past the filters.

The people who raised you—your parents, grand-parents, adoptive parents, stepparents, and/or child care providers—determined your surroundings and early experiences. Consider how the following factors influenced the family you grew up in.[2] What might you have decided about them—and about yourself? (You may find it helpful to keep a journal about what you discover and decide; having a record of your journey toward awareness can be immensely helpful.)

Your Environment

Young children have a limited experience of the world; they naturally assume that all families and all homes are like their own. When they get older, however, and begin to move in wider circles, they realize that families can be very different. Many people have reported entering the homes of friends as children and suddenly understanding that not all families were as loving (or abusive, or cold, or noisy) as their own.

Literally hundreds of variables can affect the environment in a family, and children might make hundreds of possible decisions (perceptions) based on those variables. It might help to think about the conditions in your family and the decisions you made. Did your family have a comfortable home and good food to eat, or did you grow up with poverty and deprivation? Were there

---

2. In their excellent book on personal growth, *Do It Yourself Therapy: How to Think, Feel, and Act Like a New Person in Just 8 Weeks* (Career Press, 1999), Lynn Lott, Riki Intner, and Barbara Mendenhall identify a number of factors in the environment that influence the decisions each person makes and offer more detailed suggestions about how to deal with them.

lots of people in your home or only a few? Did you come from an ethnic or cultural background that affected your ideas about men, women, and children? Did you live in a crowded city, a suburb, or a remote rural area? Were your neighbors like you in most ways or very different? What decisions did you make about yourself, your world, and what you needed to do to survive in your environment?

It could be very helpful to take some time to dig deep into your thought system and write down the decisions you have made. Note that most decisions are made at a subconscious level (or, as Adlerians would say, "beyond

> It isn't just what happens to you that is important: it's what you *decide* about what happens to you that makes a difference.

your awareness"—an important distinction because it is easier to become aware of decisions that are beyond your awareness than those that are buried in your subconscious). If you take some time to ponder, you will become aware of the decisions you made. How did your decisions influence the kind of environment you want to create for your children?

We want to emphasize again that most adults do not even consider the decisions their children are making every day of their lives together. This is a significant oversight, because these decisions are the basis of their personalities. It will take a paradigm shift for parents to begin considering the decisions their children might be making (and the eventual effect of those decisions) and patience to know that they can only guess. Exploring your own decisions will help you make this shift and will influence your future actions with your children.

Your Family's Atmosphere

Each family also has an "atmosphere," a prevailing mood that influences the people who live there. Was your family cheerful? Affectionate? Respectful? Or was the atmosphere in your home distant and chilly? Was there music playing softly, a television blaring, or dead silence? You may remember looking forward to coming home after school because you knew you would smell the aroma of cookies baking and hear people laughing in the kitchen, or you may have spent hours at a friend's home because you knew your own was filled with tears, yelling, and the crash of objects being thrown. Perhaps there was never anyone home at all. The "feeling" in a family is a powerful factor in how the members of that family react to being in it—and what they decide about themselves and others.

What decisions did you make about yourself, your world, and what you needed to do to survive in your family's atmosphere? If you have siblings, do you think your decisions differed from theirs? How did your decisions influence the kind of family atmosphere you want to create for your children? What kind of decisions do you hope your children will make?

Your Parents' Values

Parents are a child's first teachers, and the most important lessons have nothing to do with letters or numbers.

Regardless of who raised you, the adults in your life taught you "right" and "wrong" (highly subjective qualities) and modeled for you through their own behavior what was most important in life. They also passed on to you the set of "shoulds" they believed in (people "should" be honest; people "should" stick to their own kind). They may have taught you to value education, follow a particular form of spirituality, accumulate money and things, or fear people of another race or color. You learned lessons about men (they abandon their families; they yell; they have to be boss; they're kind and strong) and women (they're weak; they're nurturing; they're critical; they should obey their husbands). You learned some sort of ethics and morality and observed the character of those around you.

As we have mentioned before, sometimes the decisions people make are a form of rebellion against their parents' values. If your parents pushed religion, you may have adopted their faith—or decided to become an atheist. If you perceived your father as passive, you may have

> The "feeling" in a family is a powerful factor in how the members of that family react to being in it and what they decide about themselves and others.

looked for a "strong" partner yourself. It may take you some time to sort out what your parents believed (and exactly what you decided in response), but asking the question will open the door to a great deal of self-awareness. What decisions did you make about values? If you have siblings, do you think your decisions differed from theirs? How did your decisions influence the kind of values you want to pass on to your children? Do they seem to be accepting or rejecting your values? Is what they are doing similar to or the opposite of what you did regarding your parent's values?

Your Birth Order

It has been said that each child is born into a different family. This is why we often ask the question "Did your siblings make different decisions than you did?" While it is unwise to generalize about human behavior from only one characteristic, a number of qualities do seem to be affected by where you fit into your family of origin. Were you the oldest or the youngest? Were you somewhere in the middle? Or were you an only child? Your picture of yourself and what was required to find belonging can be deeply influenced by your birth order. It is also worth remembering that in stepfamilies—those formed when adults bring together children from past relationships— birth order often gets scrambled, which requires a great deal of mental and emotional reorganizing for children.

Detailed information about birth order is beyond the scope of this book,[3] but here are some ideas to consider. Each child, regardless of his or her position in the family, must find an answer to the questions "What must I do to belong in this family? What will make me special?" The *perceptions* children develop about their position in the family help shape their identity.

---

3. For more information on birth order, see chapter 3 of *Positive Discipline* by Jane Nelsen (Ballantine, 1996).

For firstborn children, the operative word is *first:* they're simply the first on the scene and are the recipients of their parents' entire attention and parenting energy. Oldest children often seem to be either high achievers or passionate rebels. They live in a world populated by adults and make many of their choices based on how those adults will react.

Youngest children are the "babies" and often learn to be charming manipulators of those around them; in fact, their older siblings may describe them as "spoiled." The rules have usually relaxed by the time youngest children come along, which may cause friction between these children and their older siblings. They sometimes push boundaries harder than older children because they want to have the same privileges much sooner.

Middle children often report feeling "lost in the shuffle"; they have neither the privileges of being oldest nor the special treatment of being youngest and may have to search for their own, special identity in their family. Sometimes middle children try to overcome their sense of being the "underdog" by becoming a rebel—with or without a cause.

There are many other positions for children in larger families. Wayne Frieden and Marie Hartwell Walker have written some insightful songs about seven different birth order positions.[4] One of our favorite lines from these delightful songs is "when you're somewhere in the middle of this humongous crowd."

---

4. Wayne S. Frieden and Marie Hartwell Walker, *Family Songs,* Amherst, MA: Education Research Associates (available from Empowering People Books, Tapes and Videos, 1-800-456-7770).

Your position in your family does not determine your personality. As we have noted, many factors come into play. However, what you decided about being who (and where) you were in your family constellation is an important influence. Based on your birth order, did you make any decisions similar to those described earlier? What other decisions did you make based on how you "fit" (or perceived that you didn't fit) into your family? What kind of decisions did your siblings make that may or may not fit the brief synopsis given here? Based on this information, make some guesses about what decisions your children might be making based on their birth order and how they see themselves as fitting or not fitting.

Your Parents' Parenting Styles

Whether you were raised by two parents, a single parent, stepparents, or grandparents, the adults who supervised your development and behavior had a specific approach to parenting, and much of what you have decided about raising children can be traced back to their philosophy and how you responded to it. Did they go to extremes, either of control or permissiveness? Were they abusive or neglectful? Or did they practice kind, firm parenting, setting healthy, respectful boundaries and looking for solutions (rather than blame) when problems arose?

If your own parents valued obedience and conformity above all else, you may have decided to "go along" to avoid trouble or to defy them to establish your own individuality. If your parents struggled with an alcohol or drug addiction, you have an entirely different set of feelings, thoughts, and decisions about parents and children. Now that you have children of your own, you must decide which philosophy you will adopt. You may see the importance of long-range thinking and parenting: by considering the effect your parents' approach (and your own reaction to it) has had, you can begin to make an educated decision about what "fits" for you and your children.

Many parents settle on a parenting style "by default,"

> What you decided about being who (and where) you were in your family constellation is an important influence.

doing what seems to come naturally (i.e., relying on their unconscious decisions without being aware of them) and then wondering why it doesn't work. How did you feel about your parents' parenting style? If you lived with both parents, did they have the same style? If not, how did they differ? Did you make different decisions about yourself and your world and what to do to survive depending on the parent with whom you were interacting? How do these decisions affect your parenting style with your children? Is your parenting style based on thoughtful action that is void of past decisions (highly unlikely for even the most self-aware parent), or do you more often react because of your old decisions?

Exploring your family history and the decisions you made about it gives you the tools to truly understand— and to make new decisions that *work* for you and your children. If you find that exploring your past experiences is either too difficult or too painful, you may benefit from finding a qualified therapist or a support group to help you.

Remember Maggie? She decided to find a counselor to help her resolve her anger at her mother and to understand her tendency to repeat that pattern with her own daughter. Emily went with her several times, and together they learned a great deal about where they had come from and where they wanted to go. They each realized that while they may not have chosen their childhood, they each could choose their present and have a strong influence on their children's future. That gift is available to us all.

> By considering the effect your parents' approach (and your own reaction to it) has had, you can begin to make an educated decision about what "fits" for you and your children.

Living Your Own Life, Not Your Child's Life

There is another influence on the way parents approach raising their children. Some of the unconscious decisions parents may have made along the way involve their own expectations, the unrealized dreams and goals they may have had for themselves and the expectations they have for their children. Most parents have heard stories about frustrated athletes who place footballs in an infant son's crib or would-be musicians who launch their children on music lessons at an early age. "I would never do that unless my kids wanted it," some parents are likely to declare firmly. Others may say, "What is wrong with that? I don't want my children to make the same mistakes I made." And sometimes the dreams we have for our children are so deeply rooted that we never stop to bring them into the light of day.

Is it wrong to have hopes for your young ones? Of course not—as long as your children share those hopes. Part of loving children in healthy ways is accepting who your children truly are, which may not be quite the same as who you wish they could be. Wise parents recognize that they are preparing their children for life as adults and that most people live happier, more productive lives when they are empowered to follow their own heart and their own dreams.

> Wise parents recognize that most people live happier, more productive lives when they are empowered to follow their own heart and their own dreams.

It is undeniably difficult to accept that a child does not share your values or hopes. Perhaps you've always believed in the value of a college education, while your daughter wants to join the military. You may have hobbies, interests, and sports that matter to you, while your son turns up his nose at them. You may have looked forward to grandchildren; your child announces that he or she is gay. Self-awareness and genuine love for a child often means that a parent must learn to love the child he or she actually has, regardless of whether that child fits the parent's expectations.

Children are gifts, not possessions. Just as you can't change the weather, you cannot change who your children are meant to be. You can only provide the kind of nurturing that helps them blossom into the best of what they can be (from their heart's desire, not from yours). Kahlil Gibran, in his poem *The Prophet*, captured the essence of this truth:

> *Your children are not your children.*
> *They are the sons and daughters of Life's longing for itself.*
> *They come through you but not from you,*
> *And though they are with you yet they belong not to you.*
> *You may give them your love but not your thoughts,*
> *For they have their own thoughts.*
> *You may house their bodies but not their souls,*
> *For their souls dwell in the house of tomorrow, which you*
> *   cannot visit, not even in your dreams.*
> *You may strive to be like them, but seek not to make them*
> *   like you.*
> *For life goes not backward nor tarries with yesterday.*

There is an old saying that good parenting gives a child both roots and wings. Healthy love, consistent teaching, and effective parenting skills provide the roots; having the courage to live your own dreams while freeing your children to live theirs gives them wings. Releasing children to be who they truly are may be one of the most loving things any parent can do.

CHAPTER 12

Personality

What's Your Priority?

Now that you understand the origins of your personality, you may find it helpful to explore just what it *is* and how it affects you and the people you love. There are many ways of looking at and describing human personality, and we need to recognize that it isn't helpful to limit human beings and their potential by putting them into categories and boxes. Still, having a way of describing who you have become and how you make your choices can be useful. We will focus on an approach known as *lifestyle priorities,* based on a theory developed by Israeli psychologist Nira Kefir called *impasse/priority,* which has been expanded by many Adlerian psychologists including Bill and Mim Pew, Steve Cunningham, Barbara Fairfield, and Lynn Lott.

We have repeatedly stressed the importance of recognizing the decisions that children are making about

Table 12.1   Lifestyle Priorities

Priority	Worst Fear	Believes the Way to Avoid the Worst Fear Is to:	Assets	Liabilities	Unknowingly Invites from Others:	Creates Then Complains About:
Comfort	Emotional and physical pain and stress; expectations from others; being cornered by others	Seek comfort; ask for special service; make others comfortable; avoid confrontation; choose the easiest way	Easygoing; few demands; minds own business; peacemaker; mellow; empathetic; predictable	Doesn't develop talents; limits productivity; avoids personal growth	Annoyance; imitation; boredom; impatience	Diminished productivity; impatience; lack of personal growth
Control	Humiliation; criticism; the unexpected	Control self and/or others and/or situation	Leadership; organized; productive; persistent; assertive; follows rules	Rigid; doesn't develop creativity, spontaneity, or social closeness	Rebellion; resistance; challenge; frustration	Lack of friends and closeness; feeling uptight

Table 12.1 Lifestyle Priorities (continued)

Priority	Worst Fear	Believes the Way to Avoid the Worst Fear Is to:	Assets	Liabilities	Unknowingly Invites from Others:	Creates Then Complains About:
Pleasing	Rejection; abandonment; hassles	Please others; active-demand approval; passive-evoke pity	Friendly; considerate; compromises; nonaggressive; volunteers	Doesn't check with others about what pleases them; doesn't take care of self	Pleasure at first and then resentment and rejection	Lack of respect for self and others; resentment
Superiority	Meaninglessness; unimportance	Do more; be better than others; be right; be more useful; be more competent	Knowledgeable; idealistic; persistent; social interest; gets things done	Workaholic; overburdened; overresponsible; overinvolved	Feelings of inadequacy and guilt; "How can I measure up?"; lying to avoid judgments	Being overwhelmed; lack of time; "I have to do everything"

themselves, you, and life itself. By the time you have children of your own, you have accumulated a mass of unconscious decisions and beliefs about who *you* are and what you must do to find belonging and significance. These decisions combine to form your lifestyle priority. Your priority does not describe who you are; it does describe the way you might choose to act to fulfill your primary goals of belonging and significance.

There are four lifestyle priorities: control, comfort, pleasing, and superiority. As you will notice in table 12.1, each priority has both assets and liabilities. Each priority explains how people within that personality style avoid their worst fears—the things they perceive will threaten their sense of belonging and significance. Each of us acts out of our lifestyle priority when we feel threatened or stressed or when we're confronted with change.

Our priorities are intended to protect us, but in reality the behavior motivated by each priority tends to create the opposite of what we intend. In other words, the person who chooses control to avoid criticism is often criticized for being distant and controlling. The person who chooses superiority to avoid meaninglessness often becomes so overwhelmed with tasks that he or she does not have time to enjoy meaningfulness. The person who chooses comfort to avoid stress is often stressed from trying to avoid personal growth and trying to make himself and everyone else comfortable. And the person who chooses pleasing to avoid rejection often ends up pleasing ad nauseam, feels resentful, and gets rejected. Of course, there are many different themes and ways to experience the opposite of our intentions. For example, the person with a superiority priority may get discouraged and give up instead of becoming overwhelmed.

What do lifestyle priorities look like in "real life"? Remember Maggie and Emily from chapter 11? Maggie discovered in therapy that her priority was control. She wanted more than anything to avoid criticism and humiliation and felt best about herself when she was in control of situations—a belief that created conflict with both her own mother and her strong-willed daughter. The more Maggie tried to impose on others her own sense of what was right, necessary, and important, the more resistance (and criticism) she received from those around her. As we have seen, excessive control often invites rebellion from children—and Maggie's daughter was becoming very rebellious. Not being in control made Maggie feel humiliated, which sparked her anger. Her priority also led her to resist change or situations in which she felt insecure and to withdraw when she felt threatened (silence can be a very effective form of control).

> Your lifestyle priority does not describe who you are; it does describe the way you might choose to act to fulfill your primary goals of belonging and significance.

Understanding her priority helped Maggie spot the moments when she reacted from her control style, creating mischief for herself and others. She learned to spend more time practicing the assets of her style than the liabilities. She concentrated on involving her daughter in joint decisions to avoid the power struggles. This sort of change is a slow, sometimes challenging process, but knowing your own priority gives you the information you need to spot your own "trouble areas"—and avoid them.

Discovering Your Priority

Most people have a *primary priority,* which describes what they may do when they feel threatened, and a *secondary priority,* which describes what they do when they are feeling relaxed and secure. One way of determining your primary priority is to choose which of the following statements fits you best:

- "I feel best about myself when I and those around me are comfortable and when people don't expect too much from me. I feel worst about myself when there is tension, pain, or stress." (Comfort)
- "I feel best about myself when things are orderly and organized and I am in control of myself and the situation. I feel worst about myself when I feel embarrassed and humiliated or criticized about something I think I should have known or done." (Control)
- "I feel best about myself when I can please other people and avoid conflicts so that life is pleasant, not difficult. I feel worst about myself when I feel rejected, left out, or overwhelmed by the difficulties of situations." (Pleasing)
- "I feel best about myself when I am the best I can be or when I'm achieving something important. I feel worst about myself when I feel worthless,

meaningless, and stupid, and I often compare myself to others as a measure of success." (Superiority)

The statement that is truest of you in times of stress
is your primary priority. The statement that fits when
you are feeling comfortable is likely to be your secondary priority, which is sometimes called your "operating style."

When you are in your
operating style, you will be
more rational because your
feelings are not based on fear
of a perceived threat. It is important to note that what one
personality style perceives as
threatening may be perceived
as rational by another per-

> Our priorities are intended to protect us, but in reality the behavior motivated by each priority tends to create the opposite of what we intend.

sonality style. If your operating style is control, you will
not be "controlling" (as you might be if this was your
primary style). You will operate from the assets of control rather than the liabilities and will be organized
without being rigid. If your operating style is pleasing,
you will try to please others for the pleasure of it rather
than to get something back. You will also likely be respectful enough to find out *what* pleases others instead
of deciding for yourself and then feeling resentful when
you aren't appreciated—which is how you might act if
your primary style is pleasing.

If superiority is your operating style, you are likely
to be a pleasant leader who gets things done and knows
how to involve others respectfully and to delegate so

you don't become overwhelmed. However, if superiority is your primary style, you are likely to try doing everything yourself because you don't have faith in anyone else to do it as well as you would.

If your operating style is comfort, you are a wonderful host or hostess. You know how to make people feel comfortable because you are comfortable yourself. If your primary style is comfort, you are likely to invite others to feel uncomfortable because you are trying too hard in the comfort area, but not hard enough in the risk-taking area—inviting people to think you are a bore or boring.

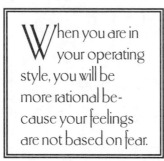

When you are in your operating style, you will be more rational because your feelings are not based on fear.

For instance, Maggie realized that when life was going smoothly, she was either using the assets of her primary style of control or her operating style of pleasing in a rational way. During these times, she found that she and Amanda got along well and rarely fought. When power struggles erupted, Maggie learned to check her lifestyle priority chart to see what mischief she might be up to. As soon as she started taking responsibility for her own behavior and apologizing for her mistakes, she found that Amanda would do the same.

Your Priority and Your Parenting

It should come as no surprise that because your own children are making unconscious decisions each day of your lives together, they also have a lifestyle priority. Your priorities (and those of your children) may fit well together, or they may clash. It is very sad that many parents invite their children to feel the very thing they themselves are trying to avoid. For example, superiority personalities may invite their children to feel inferior. Control personalities may invite their children to feel criticized. Pleasing personalities may invite their children to feel rejected ("How could you, after all I have done for you?"). Comfort personalities may invite their children to feel pain and stress because they don't help their children develop capabilities. On the other hand, children sometimes overcompensate and make entirely different decisions, as you will see in the story of Emily that follows.

Understanding the ways that you and your children (not to mention your partner) behave when feeling stressed or pressured can help you focus on solutions and communicate in healthy, effective ways. Permissive parents may discover they have a comfort or pleasing priority, while overly controlling or demanding parents may find they have a control or superiority priority. Table 12.2 will help you explore what your priority creates in your relationships with your children.

For instance, Emily, Maggie's older sister, learned that she has a primary priority of comfort; she hates stress and tension and usually finds it easier to agree with those around her and to let the rules slip a bit. Whereas Maggie confronted their mother (or withdrew into sullen silence), Emily decided simply to avoid her as well as the stress and unpleasantness that confrontations with her

Table 12.2 How Lifestyle Priorities May Influence Parenting and Caregiving

Priority	Possible Parenting Assets	Possible Parenting Liabilities	May Need to Practice
Comfort	Models for children the benefit of being easygoing, diplomatic, predictable, and enjoying simple pleasures.	Permissiveness, which may invite children to be spoiled and demanding. More interest in comfort than in the "needs of the situation."	Creating routines; setting goals; solving problems together; teaching life skills; allowing children to experience the natural consequences of their choices; family meetings.
Control	May teach children organizational skills, leadership skills, productive persistence, assertiveness, respect for law and order, time management skills.	Rigid; controlling. May invite rebellion and resistance or unhealthy pleasing.	Letting go; offering choices; asking what and how questions; involving children in decisions; family meetings.
Pleasing	May help children learn to be friendly, considerate, nonaggressive peacemakers, compromisers, volunteers, and champions of the underdog.	Doormats. Keep score (now you owe me). May invite resentment, guilt, or revenge.	Having faith in children to solve their own problems; joint problem solving; emotional honesty; learn to give and take; family meetings.

Table 12.2 How Lifestyle Priorities May Influence Parenting and Caregiving (*continued*)

Priority	Possible Parenting Assets	Possible Parenting Liabilities	May Need to Practice
Superiority	Models success and achievement; teaches children to assess quality and motivates excellence.	Lecture, preach, expect too much; invite feelings of inadequacy and failure to "measure up"; see things in terms of right and wrong instead of possibilities.	Letting go of need to be right; getting into child's world and supporting needs and goals; unconditional love; enjoying the process and developing a sense of humor; holding family meetings where all ideas are valued.

Adapted from *Positive Discipline for Preschoolers Facilitator's Guide* by Jane Nelsen, Cheryl Erwin, and Roslyn Duffy (available from Empowering People Books, Tapes, and Videos: 1-800-456-7770). For more examples of the possible effects on personality lifestyles, please see chapter 10.

created. Emily suspects that her nine-year-old son, Danny, has a superiority priority. He works hard and is a high achiever; she never has to remind him to do his homework or study for tests at school. But he is *always* right and gets frustrated when he feels he isn't getting enough recognition or when things don't happen the way he thinks they should. Sometimes Emily just feels too tired to argue with him. She disappears into her room for some cool-off time, while Danny does whatever he wants. Danny's priority and his mother's don't always mesh well.

Emily's task is to learn how to take care of herself physically and emotionally so that she feels less threatened and can be kind *and* firm with Danny when she needs to. She is also learning to use family meetings to help both of them find effective solutions to their differences and to empower Danny to use his intelligence and creativity in helpful ways.

Remember, your personality style is only one of the many factors that influence the decisions your children are making. Each child in your family may make different decisions—and have a different lifestyle priority. Gaining an understanding of personality lifestyles makes it easier to get into your children's worlds and make some guesses about the long-range effects (the decisions they may be making) of your parenting decisions, as well as the many other experiences they are having in their lives.

It can be a bit mind-boggling to consider all the beliefs, influences, and decisions that have shaped you and lead you to parent the way you do. But the time you spend will undoubtedly widen your understanding of who you are and why you do what you do. It will give you the power to change the beliefs and behaviors that are not effective in raising healthy, capable children and enable you to find new ideas and approaches that produce the results you want.

Taking Care of Yourself

In many families, the focus of attention is on the children—their activities, their behavior, their accomplishments, their needs. Parents tend to overlook the care and nurturing of the other people in the family: themselves. We've questioned the assumption many parents make that children should be the center of the family universe, but it's time to go a bit farther than mere questioning. Here's the news: your outlook on life, your relationship with the significant adults in your life, and your relationship with your children are usually only as healthy as the relationship you have with a very important person: *yourself.*

> Your outlook on life, your relationship with other adults, and your relationship with your children are usually only as healthy as the relationship you have with *yourself.*

We believe that parenting is the single most important task any of us will ever do. It takes wisdom, courage, perseverance, and an unbelievable amount of energy. We've asked you to examine the decisions, influences, and forces that shape the way you parent and have encouraged you to change the things that may not be working effectively for you. It is important to recognize that healthy changes are made by healthy people. One of the most important tasks each parent must tackle is learning to take care of her- or himself.

"Oh, sure," you may be muttering under your breath. "When am I supposed to fit that in?" Actually, taking care of yourself is not an option: it is both necessary and wise. Practicing healthy parenting skills (along with healthy marriage and relationship skills) takes time, patience, and energy. You will do your best when you are rested and healthy, both physically and emotionally.

In addition, if you are fortunate enough to have a life partner—a husband, wife, or other significant adult who shares your life—that relationship also deserves time and energy. Volumes of research show that children rely on (and learn a great deal from) the quality of their parents' relationship. Children are important, worth the best of our energy and wisdom. But grown-ups are important, too, and as we have seen already, children can learn mutual respect and cooperation when family life balances the needs of adults with the needs of children. If you are married, make spending time with your partner one of your priorities. If you are no longer married to your children's other parent, do the best you can to create a coparenting relationship that is respectful and effective. If you are a single parent, you have even more reason to nurture yourself—so much depends on you![1]

---

1. For more information on single parenting and parenting after divorce, see *Positive Discipline for Single Parents*, rev. 2d ed., Jane Nelsen, Cheryl Erwin, and Carol Delzer, Prima, 1999.

Imagine for a moment that you have in your hands a beautiful crystal pitcher filled with water. As you move through each day of your life, you pour out water from your pitcher: a splash here for your child, a dribble there for a partner or coworker, a cupful for an emergency. Parents are forever pouring out, but all too often there is little opportunity to fill the pitcher again. You care about raising healthy, happy children, or you would not be reading this book. To be an effective and loving parent, you must be a healthy person, able to respect yourself as well as those around you. In each day you should find time to nurture your inner self, to do things you enjoy, whether having a cup of coffee with a friend or soaking in a hot bubble bath by candlelight. Taking care of yourself is *not* selfishness: it is wisdom.

It's All About Balance

The journey toward health and self-awareness can be a challenging one. You may find it helpful to keep one word tucked away in the back of your mind: *balance.* Healthy parents are able to create balance: balance between work and play, kindness and firmness, caring for

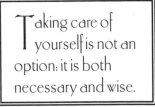

Taking care of yourself is not an option: it is both necessary and wise.

self and caring for others. We have discussed (and will undoubtedly mention again) the danger of extremes, and it is balance that keeps us centered and on the path toward the life we want for our children and ourselves. Balance, however, can be a tricky thing to find.

If you've ever tried to learn a new skill that requires balance—riding a bicycle, ice skating, or practicing yoga, to name a few—you understand how difficult finding your balance can be. As with most things in life, finding (and keeping) your balance requires awareness, effort, and practice—lots of practice. Understanding yourself as a parent, making changes when necessary, and keeping yourself and your family healthy are part of a *process*—not things that are accomplished in a single act. You will undoubtedly make mistakes and take wrong turns along the way, but remember, mistakes are always opportunities to learn and grow. You—and your children—are worth the effort.

CHAPTER 13

The Bridge to Healthy Loving

Getting Into Your Child's World

At some point in the process of raising children, parents inevitably make a fascinating (and sobering) observation. While they may have begun life as helpless little beings who are dependent on adults for guidance, teaching, and physical care, children gradually become separate individuals with their own thoughts, feelings, and personalities. Although they may resemble the parents who gave them birth ("You're *just* like your father," we say, with a mixture of fondness and exasperation), they inexorably become something altogether different. They become *themselves.*

We have repeatedly stressed the importance of long-range parenting. We have encouraged you to be aware that your children are always making decisions about how to belong, who they are, and what they must do to find significance and connection. In fact, you may already be a bit tired of hearing these phrases—and we should warn you that we're probably not finished yet. But it also may have occurred to you to wonder something rather important: if children's decisions about themselves, their parents, and life itself are so crucial to the people they are becoming, shouldn't parents know what those decisions are? How can even the most attentive and loving parent know what, precisely, their children are deciding to do, believe, and become? If healthy loving is about raising capable, competent young people who can make a contribution to their world, how can you be sure you're being an effective parent before it's too late to change? How do you get to know—*really* know—your children?

You Can't Ever Know for Sure

You can never know for sure what your children are deciding, but you can use your common sense and effective parenting skills to increase the chances that they are making healthy decisions. Children are most likely to make decisions that they are capable and competent when they are given opportunities to *feel* capable and competent. And they are likely to make unfavorable decisions about their capability if they are never given real-life opportunities to feel capable.

It's also important to understand that no two children—including siblings and even identical twins—will make exactly the same decisions. One may decide, "I am capable; therefore, I don't need any help from anyone else." Another child may decide, "I am capable; therefore, I will help others feel capable, too." Still another may decide, "I must *always* be capable; therefore, I must not make mistakes." Parenting is not easy (possibly the understatement of this or any other millennium), and understanding the decisions your children are making is not easy, either. However, when you are aware that decisions are always being made, and when you are paying attention, you can make educated guesses and then make adjustments in your parenting approach when necessary.

> Children are most likely to make decisions that they are capable and competent when they are given opportunities to *feel* capable and competent.

For example, if you get the sense that your child is becoming a perfectionist, you can emphasize that mistakes are wonderful opportunities to learn and model that view yourself. If you sense that your child is deciding she doesn't need help from anyone, you can engage in cooperation activities such as brainstorming for solutions during family meetings. If your child is acting as though she believes she is not capable, you can provide many opportunities for her to develop the belief that she is capable.

Ages and Stages

One important, but often overlooked, way of understanding children is by learning to have reasonable expectations for their behavior and abilities. You have probably heard the phrase "terrible twos" before. Did you know that the "terrible twos" really don't exist? Before you jump out of your seat in protest, let us explain. Yes, two-year-olds can be astonishingly independent. Yes, they often love the word no and delight in having different ent priorities than their frazzled parents. But it isn't personal. Despite appearances to the contrary, two-year-olds do not harbor a personal vendetta against moms and dads; they don't actually stay up nights plotting ways to frustrate and defy their parents.

> When you are aware that decisions are always being made, you can make educated guesses and then make adjustments in your parenting approach when necessary.

A two-year-old is motivated by the normal development of her body, brain, and emotions, all of which tell her to explore, learn, and experiment. She develops a working knowledge of social skills, manners, rules, and human behavior by observing adult reactions to her behavior. In other words, the average two-year-old is a mad scientist, busily conducting research experiments on her favorite laboratory subjects: her parents. Most of the parents in our workshops nod and laugh when we ask them if they didn't actually find three a more challenging age than two.

Three-year-olds bring a huge amount of physical energy to the developmental task of developing *initiative,* Erik Erikson's phrase for a child's ability to form and carry out his own plans and ideas (often creative strategies that parents find messy, dangerous, or inconvenient). One three-year-old boy we know spent days hiding with the dog in various parts of the house because he had decided to make a blanket "saddle" and ride the dog like a horse, a plan his mother, not surprisingly, didn't approve of. Three-year-olds have an uncanny knack for keeping parents on their toes, and parents are usually caught off guard: they thought *two* was supposed to be the hard part!

Why is this relevant to knowing your child? Because understanding your child's normal physical and emotional development can help you learn to respond with kindness and firmness, avoid extremes, and know why young children need teaching, routine, and consistency rather than punishment or pampering. Understanding development—whether of a toddler, a school-age child, or a teenager—allows parents to "unhook" themselves emotionally and parent in ways that encourage their children to learn the skills and attitudes they need to learn. It also eliminates a surprising amount of the anger, frustration, and hurt feelings that drive a wedge between so many parents and their children. It is downright liberating to be able to respond to a sarcastic 16-year-old calmly and firmly, rather than taking the bait, getting angry, and having yet another shouting match. It becomes easier to stay calm when you understand the impact of the physical and emotional changes that 16-year-old is experiencing and can choose not to take provocative behavior personally.

If you have never had the opportunity to learn about your child's emotional and physical development, don't wait any longer. Take a child development class or a parenting class, or read a good book. Having appropriate expectations for your child (and understanding her developmental limitations) will help you make wise parenting choices and build an excellent foundation for a relationship of mutual respect.

Time

Time and money tend to be the two things people never have enough of. Of the two, time is perhaps the most critical. Find a piece of paper and a pencil, and take a moment to consider: What are the things in your life that you believe are most important? What do you value most? What has the greatest significance? How would you like to be remembered when your life has ended? Each of us has different values and priorities; there are no hard and fast rules about what should be most important. But it is a rare parent who doesn't list "children" and "family" somewhere near the top of the list.

Now make another list. What things require your attention each week? How do you spend your time? What are all the things you "have" to do? Most adults find they spend hours at work, driving, cleaning the house, working in the yard, shopping, cooking, doing laundry, and on, and on, and on. Many are shocked to find how little time they actually spend on the things they claim are most important to them—a situation that fuels much of the guilt we discovered in chapter 6. One man in a recent workshop stood up with tears in his eyes during a discussion of priorities. "If I spent half the time on my wife and children that I spend watching television," he said sadly, "we would have a much stronger family."

Most parents these days feel guilty about something, and guilt does little good unless it leads to change. Like it or not, it is all but impossible to be close to kids without spending a considerable amount of time with them. This does not mean pampering them, nor does it mean driving them places and dropping them off; it means listening to them, hanging out with them, and paying attention to the things they do and say. It does not mean spending time controlling their every action but helping them explore the consequences of their actions. It does not mean giving in to them in the name of fun and entertainment but taking the time to help them learn how they can work and save to accomplish their own dreams and entertain themselves.

> Three-year-olds bring a huge amount of physical energy to the developmental task of developing initiative.

If you have a young child, rejoice: little ones love nothing more than to be with Mom or Dad, and you can begin now to build the sort of relationship you want to have. As children grow, their normal development takes them out of the home more often and into the world of their peers. By the time they've reached adolescence, they are far more interested in spending time with friends than with you. Still, even teenagers will accept a hamburger date once in a while or a skiing trip where you can spend hours with them in a car or on the ski lift.

Even teenagers will attend family functions (though only a limited number, and possibly with some eye rolling) when they have been respectfully involved in the planning. We know of one community that built a teen center, and the teens refused to come. We know of another community that included teens in every phase of the planning and building of a teen center—which is always crowded with teens. Children of all ages respond to respectful time spent with them.

> Like it or not, it is all but impossible to be close to kids without spending a considerable amount of time with them.

If you simply don't have any free time, consider buying a hamster. Don't have a child unless you can devote the time and energy—in healthy ways—that children have every right to expect. In the next few pages we will explore a number of ways to connect with children, understand the way they think and feel, and stay involved as they grow and change. All of these ideas will require your time; examining your priorities and learning to budget time wisely may be one of the most effective parenting decisions you will ever make.

Listening with Lips Together

Marcus fidgeted nervously with his tie as he sat on the therapist's couch. "This is the first time I've ever been in counseling," he said quietly. "I guess I'm a little uncomfortable." The therapist smiled and spoke a few encouraging words, and gradually Marcus's story began to unfold.

At the age of 32, Marcus's life was, in his words, "a mess." His wife had left the week before for an extended "visit" with her parents, taking their young daughter with her. "She's always mad at me—she thinks I'm weak. Maybe we shouldn't have gotten married in the first place," Marcus said with a sigh. He hated his job; he wanted to return to college but was afraid it was too late. And where would he find the money for school if he did decide to go?

"But the biggest problem I have is that I can't make a decision," Marcus said. "I have no confidence. No matter what I do, I'm afraid I should have done something else. Most of the time I just don't do anything at all. Maybe what I need is someone to tell me what to do all the time, like my dad used to," he finished with a wan smile.

"Your dad offered you a lot of suggestions?" the therapist asked.

Marcus snorted. "It was more like he just told me what to think and exactly what to do. I'd try to tell him about something that happened or a decision I needed to make, and he'd interrupt me before I was finished to tell me why things happened, what I should think, and what I should do about it." Marcus laughed. "He was always right, and somehow that made it worse. Sometimes I think I would rather have made mistakes on my own than have him tell me what to do all the time. I know my dad loved me a lot—he still does. But I never learned to trust my own judgment."

Marcus's father undoubtedly meant well. Sometimes it's tough being the parent. You watch your child wrestling with a problem or planning something you're almost certain won't work out. And you love your child so much, it's hard to watch him make mistakes, stumble, or get hurt. Still, one of the most loving and respectful things a parent can do is simply to listen.

Many parents listen to their children, but in truth, they're eagerly waiting for an opening in which to offer their suggestions, advice, and opinions. Parents are often right; after all, they've been around longer than their children and know more. But as Lynn Lott, one of the authors of the *Positive Discipline* books, is fond of saying, the best sort of listening is often the kind that happens with the parent's lips pressed firmly together. In other words, you listen to what your child is telling you without comment—at least until he's finished. Then it's almost always more effective to ask whether he'd like to know what you think *before* you offer suggestions.

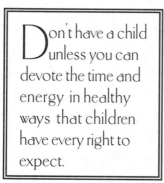

Don't have a child unless you can devote the time and energy in healthy ways that children have every right to expect.

Think back to your own childhood and adolescence for a moment. Did you enjoy being lectured? Did you find it helpful when you received unsolicited advice or criticism? Your children probably don't, either. All too often, children just decide not to talk to their parents at all. Parents "don't understand"; they "don't really listen."

One of the simplest and most powerful ways of understanding your children, learning who they are and what they think, and being aware of the choices they are making is by listening—really listening. Listen not only to the words your children say but the way they say them. Listen to their body language, their facial expressions, their behavior. We've mentioned active and reflective listening before. Mirroring your child's feelings to be sure you understand them ("You look awfully sad") is one way of helping your child feel connected and loved.

It is also helpful to listen well whenever your child is around, whether she's talking directly to you or not. Offer to drive her and her friends where they want to go, and listen to their conversation along the way. Listen when she's playing with her siblings. It's important to mention that this is *not* the same as spying, reading your child's journal, or eavesdropping on a telephone conversation (highly disrespectful forms of excessive control). Because your child *knows* you're there, she can edit her words accordingly. But sim-ply being a silent part of a conversation about what happened at school, the newest CD, or a friend's problems can tell you a lot about what your own child thinks, feels, and is deciding. If something worries or troubles you, gentle curiosity may provide you with the information you need to provide support in healthy ways.

One of the most loving and respectful things a parent can do is simply to listen.

The Power of Curiosity

These are dangerous times. Parents have good reason to worry about their children; after all, there are so many ways that children can be hurt, physically and emotionally, by the world around them. Parents worry about drugs and alcohol, about premature sexuality, about violence; they worry about the friends their children choose, about where they're going, about what they're doing once they get there.

Many loving parents let their fear rule them, and when they see their children doing something potentially damaging or dangerous, they react with overprotection, control, and judgment. But human nature being what it is, children usually respond to control and overprotection by pulling away, sneaking around, or openly rebelling, which doesn't make either parents or children feel (or do) better.

One way of responding to your child is with curiosity. The following story from *Positive Discipline for Your Stepfamily* (2nd rev. ed., Prima, 2000) shows how one mother connected with her son by choosing curiosity over judgment.

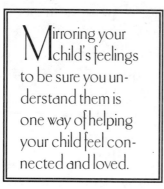

Mirroring your child's feelings to be sure you understand them is one way of helping your child feel connected and loved.

Margaret knocked on her son's bedroom door, then realized from the vibrating wood and booming bass that he couldn't hear her. Alex, 14, had his favorite hip-hop music turned up as loud as it would go—again.

"Turn that down!" Margaret shouted, as she opened the door. "Dinner's ready! Why must you have that up so loud? I don't know how you can listen to it—it's obscene," she finished grumpily and then felt a twinge of guilt as she saw the hurt in Alex's eyes.

"What's up, Meg?" her husband Mark asked as she stalked back into the kitchen.

"Alex is listening to that rap stuff again," she said. "I hate it—the language is awful and it glorifies crime. I don't like the way it talks about women, either. I've thought about forbidding him to listen to it, but all of his friends do. He'll just listen when he's with them. I know he's a good kid, but why does he like such horrible music?"

Mark grinned. "That's how our folks used to feel about the Beatles and the Rolling Stones, remember? And how their folks felt about Frank Sinatra. Or the way older people felt about the waltz back in Vienna when it first arrived. Scandalous!" He reached out and gave his wife a squeeze. "Have you ever talked calmly with Alex about it?"

Margaret shook her head sheepishly. "No, I just lecture and nag him about it. He's lucky to have a stepdad like you, honey. I'd probably drive him crazy all by myself."

Several days later, Margaret was driving home from the mall with Alex, who had used his birthday money to buy a new CD. "You know, Alex," Meg said thoughtfully, "I've been pretty hard on you about your music. And I'm wondering why you like rap—or is it hip-hop?—so much. Could you put your new CD on the car player and maybe explain it to me?"

"Are you crazy, Mom?" Alex blurted out. Then, more softly, "You know you hate my music. Besides, it has the 'f' word in it."

"I've heard that word before," Margaret said with a laugh. "Just be sure you don't ever say it to me! Anyway, I want to understand you, Alex. When I was your age, my parents complained about my music but they would never actually listen to it. It used to make me mad. I guess I don't want to treat you the same way. Why don't you play the tune you like the best?"

"Well, okay," Alex said uncertainly. "But you won't like it."

He was right—Margaret didn't. But as they listened, she asked Alex to explain to her what things he liked about the music and that particular artist. She asked him how the music made him feel, and she listened carefully to his answers. On the way home from the mall, Meg and her son had a fascinating and wide-ranging conversation about prejudice, race, attitudes toward women, drugs, and teen behavior.

As they pulled into the driveway and Alex removed his CD, he looked over at his mother. "Mom, I hope you know that just because I listen to this music, I'm not going to go out and do drugs or something. I just like the beat. And I know the difference between right and wrong."

"I know you do, Alex. Thank you for sharing your music with me. I learned a lot."

A few days later, Alex presented his mother with a special gift. Looking just a little embarrassed, he handed her a CD with a hand-lettered label. "I made this for you on Dad's CD burner when I was at his house last weekend," he said. "It's some of my favorite music for you to have."

Margaret took the CD and gave Alex a hug, recognizing that he had offered her a place in his heart and life. "Thanks," she said, meaning it sincerely. "This means a lot to me."

Will Margaret ever truly love rap music? Probably not. But by showing curiosity about her son's interest rather than judging it, she was able to open a door between them. What could have become an issue that divided them became instead a way to communicate and connect.

Closet Listening

"Closet listening" means listening without it being obvious that that is what you are doing. Many parents complain, "I try to listen, but my child won't talk to me." Often children won't talk because what seems like loving interest to you feels like the third degree to them. They don't want to tell you about their school day on cue: "How was school today?" However, if you find ways to listen without asking questions, you will be surprised how much you hear. You might sit down for cookies and milk after school. In many cases, your child will soon be talking about her day—without being asked.

Mrs. Fisher used to go into the bathroom and sit on the edge of the tub while her daughter primped for school. At first her daughter asked, "What do you want?" Mrs. Fisher replied, "I just enjoy spending time with you." Soon her daughter took it for granted that her mother would be there (not saying a word) and chatted away about her life while she got ready for school. Of course, you don't always have to keep your mouth shut to be a good listener. However, you do need to learn how to avoid lectures.

Expressing Curiosity with "What" and "How" Questions

As we explained in chapter 9, we're not talking about interrogating your child. What and how questions, when asked with curiosity and genuine interest rather than judgment or suspicion, can be a marvelous and effective way of connecting with your child and understanding how he sees his world. As we've also seen, they have the added benefit of encouraging children to learn to think for themselves, develop perceptions of capability, and solve problems. Curiosity does not mean you agree with your child's choices (Margaret, it is clear, will never truly love rap music), but you invite your child to draw closer to you when you show interest in why *he* likes the things he likes or has made the choices he's made. Curiosity and interest make a much better foundation for setting boundaries and limits, or for working on solving problems together, than do judgment and lectures.

> If you find ways to listen without asking questions, you will be surprised how much you hear.

How might your child respond to these questions? (Remember, attitude is everything!)

- What things do you like about that movie (or TV show, or music)?
- How do you feel when you're with that group of friends?
- What is it about _____ (fill in name of least desirable friend) that you really like?
- Can you show me how to play that video game? (We know—this one didn't start with "what" or "how." But the attitude of curiosity is more effective than the words themselves.)

Share Your Own History

Curiosity can work the other way around, too. In this media-dominated world, children often know far more about their favorite television characters, celebrities, and athletes than they do about their own parents. Another effective way of connecting with kids is to share your own history and experiences with them. No, this doesn't mean hauling out the old lectures about "When I was your age, I walked eight miles through the snow to school" or "When I was your age, I didn't have a car at all. I had to ride the bus, and it didn't do me any harm." Sometimes the most loving thing you can offer a hurting child is the recollection of a time when you felt the same way.

Having a history and a heritage is important to children. Knowing who their parents are (and that they are quite human) can give children a more solid sense of themselves. We spent some time in chapter 9 talking about the importance of family meetings; perhaps sharing old photographs and mementos, telling old family stories (especially the times you got in trouble—kids *love* those stories), and talking about where your family came from can become part of your family meetings or your holiday rituals. Take your children to work with you if you can; share your hobbies and interests. As always, the key word is *invite,* not *force.* Knowing you welcome their presence often makes children more interested in being with you.

Spend Special Time

There's that word again. Parenting definitely takes a lot of time. And it's important to have one-on-one time, time without distractions, noise, and crowds, to spend with each child in your life. We call these moments "special time," and children crave them. Special time need not cost money; it isn't always about providing fun or making children happy. Special time can be as simple as doing a task together ("Hey, kiddo, want to see what a car engine looks like?"), reading a story, or going for a walk. Special time may be part of your bedtime routine, or it may happen in the car on the way to school or soccer practice. It may mean having a

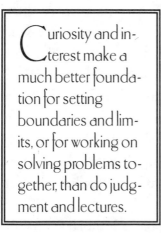

Curiosity and interest make a much better foundation for setting boundaries and limits, or for working on solving problems together, than do judgment and lectures.

DENNIS THE MENACE

"DO I HAVE TO DO ALL OF THE PLAYING AROUND HERE?"

DENNIS THE MENACE® used by permission of Hank Ketcham and © by North American Syndicate.

special lunch or shopping trip with each child. Special time is "just us, Mom" or "just us, Dad" time. It's probably obvious that it happens best when it's been planned and budgeted for. Listening and curiosity become much easier to practice when you're able to focus on one child at a time—and when you've created time to do it.

Special time doesn't need to take hours and hours. A few minutes that happen regularly may be all you need. You may find that a few moments of special time have a powerful effect on your child's sense of belonging and significance—and on your sense of connection to him. Listening, curiosity, and special time are not intended to increase your control over your child—we've already seen time and time again that control (or permissiveness) is not the answer. Connecting with children is about knowing who they are and what they are deciding, so that you can solve problems, set limits, and face the risks of the future *together.*

Beware the Anger Trap

Let's admit it: all parents get angry. We love to ask workshop audiences whether anyone has never been angry with a child. People giggle uncomfortably, look around nervously—and realize that *no one* has raised a hand. Anger may be a normal part of living with children, but it can be destructive. Anger sometimes keeps even the most loving and thoughtful parents from doing their best work when they most need to—under pressure.

Andrew learned this lesson the hard way. Andrew was 28 when he married Tabitha and adopted her three children. As he told his parenting group, "I went from being a fun-loving single guy to the father of three little kids, and I couldn't figure out why there was always stuff all over the place!" Andrew knew very little about child development or discipline; he parented "by the seat of his pants." He admitted that he probably had unrealistic expectations. As the years passed, Andrew's relationship with his three stepchildren became more and more hostile. Andrew was excessively controlling; Tabitha compensated (and tried to protect her children) by being too permissive. He would command, direct, and expect; the children would resist, withdraw, and rebel. He couldn't believe their lack of respect, they couldn't stand the way he talked to them, and Tabitha felt caught in the middle. The entire family was unhappy.

After one particularly heated encounter, Andrew and Tabitha joined a parenting class. They worked hard, and Andrew in particular learned how to listen to his children, how to enter their world, and how to invite cooperation. Then came the inevitable bad day. The oldest child, a 10-year-old girl, failed to clean up her room adequately. Andrew lost his temper. "Go to your pigsty of a room," he shouted. "I don't want to see your ugly face out here."

> Special time need not cost money; it isn't always about providing fun or making children happy.

As he told his parenting group sadly the next week, "We're back to square one. I'll start over and I'm sure things will get better, but how I wish I'd kept my mouth shut. I can still see the look on her face, and it breaks my heart."

One angry outburst will not ruin your relationship with your children, and there are times when parents are entitled to feel angry and frustrated. But what you *feel* can (and often should) be different than what you *do*. Harsh words, especially those that wound a young heart, lodge themselves in the memory and can be abominably hard to erase. Time-out is one discipline tool that is usually best used by parents—on themselves! It can take months, even years, to build a relationship of connection and respect; it sometimes takes only one angry moment to damage it.

If you've blown it—and who among us hasn't—remember that mistakes are opportunities to learn. You can apologize to your child, explore what happened, and find solutions together to avoid future problems. Believe it or not, when resolved with dignity and humility, even an argument can become a bridge to greater closeness.

Have Faith in Your Child and Learn to Let Go

Many loving parents believe that effective parenting is about knowing *where* your children are—what they're doing, who they're with, and when, and where. We believe that it is more important to know *who* your children are than just *where* they are. Knowing who your children are gives you the security and the faith to let

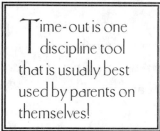

Time-out is one discipline tool that is usually best used by parents on themselves!

them learn, let them try new things (and make mistakes) in a supportive environment, and let them become the people they truly are. There will be times when you feel wonderfully close to your children and other times when they seem distant and even hostile. For instance, understanding development will tell you that teenagers insist on privacy. It isn't personal; it's just what they need at that stage of their lives. What matters is keeping the door (and your ears) open, having the time to spend with them, and being genuinely interested in the way they see the world around them.

Being invited into a child's world is a fascinating and truly educational experience—and you can't force your way in. Like it or not, children determine when and whom they will trust, when they will speak, and what they will say. Wise parents learn to offer a little space, some understanding and encouragement, and the time to listen. You can find time to play with kids (yes—you, too, can play Barbies and Legos) and be available. You can remember that you only get one chance to share their childhood with the children you love so deeply.

Ultimately, a parent's job is to teach, guide, and encourage, and then to let go in loving, appropriate ways. The letting go is always a little scary; it becomes less so when you know who your children are and what they are capable of. You will know that far better when you are able to get into their world and stay a while and to truly connect with the interesting, capable people they are becoming.

CHAPTER 14

No More Extremes
(At Least Hardly Ever)

Kind and Firm Parenting in Action

By now you may be concluding that you have loved your children too much. Like us, you may be all too aware of the times you haven't practiced long-range parenting, the times you've given in to the almost irresistible urge to control or to pamper, and the mistakes you've made with your children in the name of love. We all do it. And even forearmed with education and experience, we're likely to do it again. That is why it is so encouraging to know that mistakes truly are opportunities to learn.

But parenting takes place in the real world, not in the pages of a parenting book or magazine. You have real, flesh-and-blood children with strengths and a few weaknesses. They will make mistakes and wrong choices (and, like the rest of us, have occasional bad days); you will, too. The goal of parenting is not perfection but to raise children to become capable, competent adults who can lead successful, happy lives in spite of their mistakes—or perhaps even because they have learned how to recover from mistakes. In other words, your job as a parent is to become dispensable. You will always be there to provide love and support, but you will no longer be in charge.

Children, even the most beloved of them, can be enormously frustrating, and old patterns and beliefs are sometimes hard to change. You may be willing to concede that the extremes of parenting—excessive control and permissiveness—don't work in the long term, but what does? How does kind and firm parenting look in action, on real problems?

Parenting in the Real World

One of the blessings of moms' groups and parenting classes is the opportunity to learn that you're not alone. Most parents find it reassuring to hear other parents talk about their problems and questions. It becomes apparent rather quickly that families often struggle with many of the same issues.

For instance, if you have young children (younger than three or four), you have probably learned by now that there are three things you just can't make toddlers do (although many parents try their best just the same). Those things are eating ("Open wide, here comes the choo-choo" or "No dessert for you if you don't finish your vegetables!"), sleeping ("Okay, you can sleep with Mommy and Daddy just one more night" or "Turn out the light and get back into bed this *in*stant, young man!"), and toilet training ("Grandma says all *her* children were potty trained by 18 months" or "I'll buy you that Poké-mon game if you'll poop in the potty just once").

Children have absolute control of their bodies. A parent's job is to set the stage, teach the appropriate skills, and relax and let children do their job. Most parents, even the most nervous, eventually figure out that children never go off to kindergarten in diapers. We won't spend a great deal of time on these subjects be-cause they've been covered in great detail elsewhere (if you have an urgent need to know more, check out *Positive Discipline: The First Three Years* and *Positive Discipline for Preschoolers*). We do want to take a closer look at some of the issues that cause so much conflict and confusion in families with older children, the "big three" of everyday parenting: money, chores, and homework. How can parents ap-proach these problems in healthy ways? How do you create cooperation, set appropriate expectations and limits, and follow through when necessary? What does this kind and firm stuff really look like, anyway?

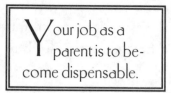

Your job as a parent is to be-come dispensable.

Money, Money, Money

It may not be the root of all evil, but money (and whether to give it to children, and how, and for what purposes) certainly causes more than its share of misery for families. By the standards of the rest of the world, most Americans are quite comfortable, even affluent. American children have a significant voice in how their parents spend their money ("Buy me that, Daddy!"), and many children have quite a bit of spending money of their own. This is one of the many areas where loving too much can be more hurtful than helpful because instead of gratitude, children seem to develop an attitude of "more, more, more." And (yes, we are saying it again) a key consideration in all your parenting methods is to understand the decisions your children are making and how those decisions affect their personalities and behavior.

Banks and lending institutions, of course, are well aware of how much spending is influenced by young people. Many parents report receiving letters from banks inviting them to "begin early to build a good credit rating for your child" and offering low-limit credit cards to high school and college students. Young adults who have never been taught to appreciate the value of a dollar (or how to earn one) often accumulate staggering amounts of credit card debt. Sadly, a number have even committed suicide because they felt unable to deal with their debts.

> A parent's job is to set the stage, teach the appropriate skills, and relax and let children do their job.

One high school teacher showed a film to his students about a young married couple who found themselves deeply in debt because they charged everything they wanted on their credit cards—cars, clothes, furniture, fancy meals. The teacher stopped the film to engage his students in a discussion about the couple's predicament and ask for their opinion about what the couple should do to solve this problem. The overwhelming conclusion was "They should go to their parents for help." This, unfortunately, is typical thinking for children of parents who love too much. It simply did not occur to this couple (or to the high school students viewing their story) to take responsibility for the mess they had created, nor did it occur to them that they could stop spending and work very hard to pay off their credit card debt, even though it might take a long time.

Acquiring and managing money are issues for most adults these days, so it isn't surprising that they struggle to figure out financial issues with their children. (Interestingly enough, money is often closely linked to another of the big issues: chores. But we'll look at that more closely in a few pages.) When money becomes the issue, many loving parents resort to the extremes we've explored. Let's take a look at two real-life examples.

Jay is 17. His mother enrolled him in a juvenile justice counseling program because he had been stealing money from her purse and she feared he would eventually begin stealing from others.

"Why do you steal, Jay?" the juvenile officer asked.

Jay looked out sullenly from under the brim of his cap. "Because I need money," he said curtly. "And I never have any." Warming to his subject, he sat up straighter and anger seeped into his voice. "I always have to borrow money from my friends for lunch and rides. It isn't fair for them to have to pay my way. I can't afford to go to a movie or go hang out at the burger place."

"Have you considered getting a job?" the officer asked gently.

"I'd love to," Jay retorted, "but there isn't anyplace to work near our house, and she won't let me drive." He shot a bitter look at his mother, who bristled defensively.

"Jay can drive when he can pay for his gas and insurance," she said firmly. "And he gets an allowance. I just happen to believe that money should be earned, and he never earns his."

As it turned out, Jay's mother did give him an allowance of $15 a week. But each time he failed to do a chore or made a mistake—leaving a sock on the floor, forgetting to mow the lawn, coming home late, leaving crumbs on the counter—a dollar was deducted. Money also was deducted when his grades weren't good enough. All told, it had been more than five months since Jay had received any of his allowance. He was willing to work but couldn't get to a job because he had no money to pay for gas and insurance; he couldn't earn that money because he couldn't work. As time passed he felt more and more frustrated, stuck, and defiant. Even when he tried to do all of his chores, there always seemed to be something he forgot, something that wasn't good enough. Eventually, the simplest way out of his dilemma seemed to be stealing money from his mother.

Stealing is never okay. But Jay's frustration is understandable. Jay's mother loved him; she believed she was teaching him to handle money responsibly. Trouble was, he had few acceptable ways of acquiring money to handle.

At the Opposite Extreme

Brandon, on the other hand, has no need to steal. Brandon also is 17. His father started a successful chain of convenience stores and could (and usually did) buy Brandon anything he wanted. Brandon's dad was a busy guy and didn't get to spend as much time with his son as he would have liked. Brandon had a lot of free time and a *lot* of spending money. On his sixteenth birthday, he received a new Jeep. Brandon selected a personalized plate ("LOVRBOY") and promptly wrecked the Jeep driving home drunk from a party.

Brandon's father gave him a stern lecture—and bought him a new pickup truck. Brandon drove that truck for about six months before he wrecked it. This time he got a much longer lecture—and a new Camaro. At 17, Brandon has made some valuable observations: Dad has bottomless pockets, not enough time, and no desire to follow through on his lectures. Brandon's life is one long party.

Jay's mother used excessive control to "teach" him about money; Brandon's father pampered him. Neither approach is a good choice for the long term: neither Jay nor Brandon's decisions about themselves and about life are likely to help them learn to earn money or manage it wisely. They are not developing a sense of belonging; they feel little or no sense of *healthy* personal power, nor are they developing much compassion for those around them.

How do you teach children about money? Shouldn't it be earned by doing chores? What does kind and firm parenting look like when it comes to money matters?

What About an Allowance?

Providing an allowance is a tool parents can use to teach children many valuable lessons about money. After all, children can't learn to manage money if they never have any. Too many parents give "handouts" instead of fixed allowances. Handouts are often based on the whims of parents and/or the ability of kids to coax, whine, and manipulate. (By the way, kids usually believe that checks, credit cards, and ATMs provide an unlimited supply of money and rarely believe you "can't afford it" when they see you pulling dollar bills out of a machine.)

Fixed allowances are decided upon in advance and are distributed *only* once a week. Giving monetary handouts is a very disrespectful system that leaves everyone feeling bad: parents who feel manipulated by coaxing, crying, or other demands for money (which is never appreciated by their children) and children who do not learn the confidence and self-respect that comes from dealing responsibly with money. Set allowances provide children with the opportunity to budget money and experience the consequences of unwise spending— namely, running out of money before the week is over.

Allowances can be started when children first become aware of the need for money, usually when they start wanting toys at the supermarket or treats from the ice cream truck. Some families start with a quarter, a dime, a nickel, five pennies, and a piggy bank. A small child loves the variety and enjoys putting the money in the piggy bank. As children get older, allowances can be based on need. Children learn budgeting when parents take time to go over their needs with them. A child of six may need $0.25 for gum and $0.25 for savings. A child of 15 may need $7.00 a week for a movie, $5.00 for school lunches, and $4.00 for savings or snacks.

If kids run out of money before the end of the week, it is important to empathize but not rescue. Children also can learn from the consequences of their decisions when they have the freedom to spend their allowance as they wish. If they spend it all at once, they have the opportunity to learn from that experience, as long as parents don't interfere or make judgments.

This does not mean that allowances cannot be renegotiated. Renegotiation is an important part of the learning process as kids get older and their needs change. Birthdays or the start of a new school year are good times to sit down together, look at needs, and go over budget planning.

A clothing allowance is a good addition to a regular allowance as soon as kids are old enough to be aware of fashion and want more clothing than is really necessary. A clothing allowance provides limits and encourages responsible decision making. Younger children may need two shopping trips each year, one in the spring and one in the fall, each with a certain dollar amount allotted. As children get older, they may get a certain amount each month to budget.

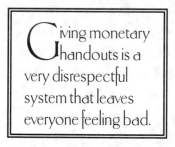

Giving monetary handouts is a very disrespectful system that leaves everyone feeling bad.

The allowance system is respectful to all concerned. It is negotiated in advance based on what the family can afford and on the kids' needs. If the children's needs are greater than the family budget, they can be encouraged to supplement their income by baby-sitting, washing cars, or mowing lawns. (No, the allowance should not be tied to chores. More about that in a page or two.) When an allowance is agreed on, your responsibility is to do what you have promised and to follow through when necessary with kind and firm action. Let's take a look at how this system works in action.

Kind and Firm Finances

Kevin grew up with a single mom. Jackie didn't have a lot of extra money to spend when her son was small, but she wanted Kevin to have the things he wanted *and* to learn to handle what he had. Jackie began giving Kevin an allowance when he was six. (She decided not to tie the allowance to chores.) It wasn't much—only $1.00 a week—and as with most six-year-olds, the money burned a hole in Kevin's small pockets. Every time Jackie and Kevin went to the store, he spent his allowance on a small toy or a pack of baseball cards. Later in the week, when he begged to rent a video game or buy some more baseball cards, his mom would smile and say, "That's what your allowance is for. Do you have any money left?"

Kevin would pout and occasionally beg; Jackie would agree that it's disappointing not to have the things you want and encourage him to wait for next week's allowance. Eventually Kevin figured out that if he actually saved his dollar for a few weeks, he could afford something *really* cool. As he grew, Jackie slowly increased his allowance. She never forced him to put his money in the bank, nor did she give him money just because he wanted it. When Kevin whined ("All my friends get $5.00 a week!"), she invited him to join her as she paid the monthly bills.

Jackie showed her son how much she earned each month and explained the rent and utility payments. (Kevin was astonished to learn that you actually had to *pay* for electricity and to flush the toilet.) They talked about clothing, car expenses, food, and possible medical and dental expenses (Kevin would need braces on his teeth). Jackie showed Kevin how much it cost for him to be in Little League and Boy Scouts. Jackie was careful not to lecture; she simply explained and invited Kevin to offer suggestions and ideas.

Kevin, being a very human young man, still occasionally whined and wanted things he couldn't have. But he did understand his mother's position and was proud of how hard she worked. By the time Kevin was 17, he had a job (only three days a week, because school had to come first) and was driving a truck (not new, but he loved it all the same) that he had paid for himself. He kept some of his money to spend on music, dates, a sound system for his truck, and special articles of clothing, but he put a surprising amount in the bank. Jackie laughingly told friends that Kevin always had more cash than she did!

Jackie had decided early to be both kind and firm with Kevin about money. He had some of his own from the very beginning, but he learned (usually from his own mistakes) that once spent, it was gone forever.

Jackie didn't allow "borrowing" against the allowance. Because she was able to set firm limits and follow through with kindness, Kevin was able to learn with only a little argument and hassle to earn and to save on his own. His mom helped him when she felt it was appropriate (she might agree to pay half of a really big purchase, such as a bike), but she did not rescue him. Jackie also used practical experience to teach (not lecture) Kevin about the real world of money, its limitations, and its possibilities.

What do you want your children to learn about money? (Incidentally, what are they learning from the way you handle money? Recent statistics indicate that saving, particularly for retirement, is at an all-time low in this country, while consumer spending and credit card debt remain disturbingly high.) How will they learn to earn, save, invest, and spend wisely? Remember, discipline is about teaching. Consider the skills and knowledge your children will need in the future, then make an effort to incorporate those concepts into your daily life as a family. Yes, it takes patience, thought, and planning—but the results are well worth it.

Chore Wars

When children are little, they love to grab the vacuum, scrub the bathroom, pull weeds out of dirt, and wash dishes in the sink. When they splash and make puddles, they even love to be handed a sponge and invited to mop up. So what happens once they turn six or seven? If there are older children out there who love to do house and yard work, they are rare indeed. By the time they're teenagers, getting them to do chores is a monumental undertaking. No wonder so many parents find it easier just to do it themselves.

The truth is that chores aren't a high priority item on the agenda of most children. Admit it: you'd worry a bit about a 10-year-old who would rather clean up his room than play with friends. Since few adults enjoy doing chores, it shouldn't surprise anyone that kids don't like them either. Still, pitching in and helping out is part of being a family. Life becomes smoother, easier, and a lot more fun when everyone pulls his or her weight.

Chores and Allowances: No Connection

Somewhere in the misty past of parenting, someone had the bright idea of tying money to chores. "Kids hate chores; kids want money. Therefore," the reasoning goes, "we'll give kids money only if they do chores!" Seems simple, right? Yet how many family arguments have begun over who did which chores, whether they got done correctly (and on time), and how much they're worth? Many families have created elaborate job and allowance charts, complete with stickers, and found themselves scrapping the entire system because it became such a hassle.

Many problems can be avoided when allowances are not tied to chores. A four-year-old may enthusiastically make her bed for $0.10 but will ask for $0.50 by the time she is eight. By the time she is 14, she won't want to do it even for a dollar. Connecting chores to allowances offers too many opportunities for punishment, reward, bribery, and other forms of disrespectful manipulation. Each child gets an allowance just because he or she is a member of the family, and each child does chores just because he or she is a member of the family. It can be helpful to offer special jobs for pay that are beyond regular chore routines, such as weeding for $2.00 an hour or cracking nuts for $1.00 a bag. This offers opportunities for kids who want to earn extra money but does not cause problems if they choose not to take the opportunity.

The problem with the "pay children for helping out" philosophy is that children don't have the opportunity to learn that there are some things you do just to do your part. (It is called cooperation and contribution.) They also don't learn that there are some things you do, even though you don't like having to do them, simply because your life works

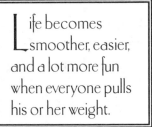

Life becomes smoother, easier, and a lot more fun when everyone pulls his or her weight.

better when they are done. Instead, children learn always to expect a monetary pay-off, not only for chores but also for grades and achievement. Many parents argue that they receive monetary payment for their employment. However, we have never seen a truly happy person who worked *only* for monetary gain. Very few people make significant advances in their workplace without enthusiasm for hard work, cooperation, and problem-solving skills—attitudes and skills children learn when they are respectfully involved (through family meetings) in deciding what, when, and how chores should be done.

Instead, the extremes of parenting come into play around the issue of chores. Some parents try the drill-sergeant approach: they issue commands and refuse to allow children to watch television or go outside until their rooms are clean; children either ignore them, argue with them, or respond with classic passive-aggressive behavior. When children hear lectures and put-downs

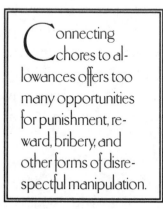

Connecting chores to allowances offers too many opportunities for punishment, reward, bribery, and other forms of disrespectful manipulation.

about their lack of enthusiasm about chores, they get defensive, resistant, or defiant. When they feel they can't resist any longer, they can at least do as little as possible.

Does the following encounter sound familiar to you?

Parent: Pick up your shoes, or you can't play on the computer!

Parent (twenty minutes and lots of grumbling later): Hey, you didn't pick up your socks!

Child: You didn't *say* "socks"!

Parents may believe that children should be having fun or that it's just too hard to get them to cooperate. So, loving parents (usually it's Mom) pick up after their children, do their laundry, wait on them ("Hey, Mom, can you bring me a soda?"), and prepare their favorite foods, and then wonder grumpily why children never do anything for themselves. We have a simple response: Why should they when they have you? We keep coming back to kindness and firmness at the same time. This approach can make it less distasteful for children to do something that isn't at the top of their priority list but that still needs to be done.

The Family That Works Together . . .

A research study once found that seven out of ten times, people will offer their cooperation when asked respectfully. (Notice that it's not ten out of ten times!) Paying children an allowance to participate in family work is a form of bribery that effectively eliminates the opportunity for them to learn helpfulness and cooperation "just because."

Chores and allowances should be two separate issues. Children seem to learn the values and lessons parents intend them to learn best when the two issues are not tied together. Chores and household work are simply part of being a family. No one pays Mom and Dad to do chores around the house; children also can contribute and cooperate (and learn social interest and practical life skills in the process) just because they're part of the family. Being both kind and firm will help a great deal.

The firm part comes from knowing what you want to achieve. It is reasonable to expect children to help out, not only because they share the benefits of living in your home but also because they will need to know these skills someday to live on their own.

Your children's ages and abilities are a critical part of this process. Expecting "help" from children that they are not developmentally ready to give will only frustrate both of you. For example, a four-year-old can easily clean her room when the task is broken down into simple steps: "Can you pick up the books?" "How about the Barbies?" You can even work alongside and help her. (Remember, teaching the skills is part of getting a good

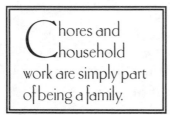

Chores and Chousehold work are simply part of being a family.

result.) But turning that same four-year-old loose and saying, "Clean your room!" will probably get you nowhere. She isn't old enough to understand exactly what you mean by that, nor does she have the perseverance or the attention span to stick with the job until it's done. An older child is capable of doing the task much more capably. Always be sure your child has the physical and emotional maturity to do the job you're asking her to do.

The kind part means recognizing that, as our grandparents used to say, "You catch more flies with honey than with vinegar." It isn't necessary to use a harsh voice to get cooperation; in fact, cooperation usually happens best when smiles are present. Doing chores together, believe it or not, can actually be fun. Some families find that taking fifteen minutes each day to do family work together eliminates the all-day-Saturday drudgery everyone hates. For more detailed information on settling your chore conflicts, we highly recommend *Chores Without Wars* by Lynn Lott and Riki Intner (Prima, 1998).

Regardless of the approach you choose, beware of extremes and focus on the long-range results you want for your children. Your kids will probably continue to hate doing them, but chores need not be the torture they so often become.

Homework Hassles

Homework is right up there at the top of the list of things kids hate, right along with chores. And, like chores, homework is something kids just have to do—although we confess, we sometimes don't see the point. The amount of real learning that takes place because children do worksheets and essays at home is suspect. Still, teachers go on giving homework and parents go on expecting it, which means that children will have to go on doing it and turning it in. The problem is that, like chores, a child would rather be doing a million things other than homework, especially after having spent six hours in class (an occupation that many children find painfully "boring"—especially when compared with video and computer games, television, and active play). Loving parents, in the interests of supporting education and "helping" their children excel, often find themselves being excessively controlling or incredibly permissive when it comes to their child's homework. Consider these stories (once again, borrowed from real-life parents).

Nancy believes that school is important. In fact, succeeding in school is her top priority for her two children,

Jordan and Megan. Good grades come easily to eight-year-old Megan, a bright, confident youngster, but for 10-year-old Jordan, school is a discouraging torment that happens almost every day of his life. Academics aren't easy for him; he is gifted in art but gets to spend very little time on that subject. His teacher hands out lots and lots of homework assignments. Jordan has to write them all down and present his weekly homework planner to his mother, who promptly takes charge.

Nancy believes that homework should be done first, so Jordan isn't allowed to go out and play until every last bit is finished. There is no TV; no snacks or distractions are allowed until the reading, spelling, and studying are done. Nancy sits at the table with Jordan (Megan has long since finished her work and gone off to play with friends) and nags, lectures, and prods him through his work, which he stubbornly claims not to understand. Homework can—and often does—take two or three hours each day to complete. Jordan forgets his assignments, misplaces his books, and refuses to concentrate. When the work is done, he "forgets" to turn it in on time. His teacher sends daily notes to Nancy listing the things that need to be done; Nancy issues orders to Jordan about collecting supplies and following through and asks him why he can't be more like Megan. Nancy is frustrated and angry; Jordan is terminally discouraged.

Then there is Cassie. Cassie is nine years old. She hates homework, too, but has found another way of avoiding it. Cassie "can't": she weeps and whines and has convinced her parents that her schoolwork is just too hard for her. So, to help her get by, Cassie's busy parents asked her grandmother, a retired teacher, to come over every afternoon and supervise her homework. In actuality, Grandma pretty much does it all: she corrects spelling, writes out the math problems, and dictates sentence structure. Cassie scribbles obediently while watching her favorite after-school shows on TV. Cassie's grandma and her parents love her very much and are happy that they can help her "succeed."

Cassie's parents believe things are going pretty well—after all, her grades are acceptable and she has few behavior problems—until her parent-teacher conference. Cassie, the teacher tells them, cannot do her own work. She sits next to children who will let her copy their papers and has become adept at reading others' work upside down. Cassie is getting by, but she is learning nothing—except how to manipulate others into doing her work for her.

Jordan's mother, in an effort to help her struggling son, has resorted to excessive control, and Jordan is resisting her every way he can, growing more and more discouraged by the moment. He is not learning skills or attitudes that will help him succeed in other areas of his life. Cassie's parents and grandmother are pampering her, doing her work for her in an effort to encourage and help her—and, possibly, because it seems like the easiest way to get through it. Cassie isn't learning confidence or competence; she has decided that the best way to tackle a difficult job is to get someone else to do it for her. Neither child is headed for a promising school career, or, unfortunately, for the sort of skills and beliefs that lead to an effective adult life.

Lack of Motivation

Q: I am writing for help with a situation with my nine-year-old son. He is in the fourth grade and is gifted. He is a very bright child but often is unmotivated to do more than the minimum to get by. He is also very unorganized and often forgets to bring his homework sheets or books home from school. This frustrates me as a parent, because I do not know what to do to help him. He gets a logical consequence at school when he doesn't have his homework (misses recess), but what can I do as a parent to help him be more responsible and motivate him to always do his best?

A: The best way to help your child be responsible is for you to be consciously irresponsible. In other words, why should he be responsible when you have that area all sewed up? Don't you feel resentful when another person tries to tell you what you should do? That is enough to make most of us rebellious.

You are not truly helping your son by trying to micromanage everything he does. It is time for you to let go—and to know that letting go does not mean abandonment. You can show empathy without rescuing. When he loses his recess, you can show empathy, *period.* You might be surprised how much more motivated he may become when you stop trying to motivate him.

Another possibility is to help him explore the consequences of his choices without lecturing. You do this by asking "curiosity questions," which means you must be curious instead of trying to get him to say what you want him to say. You can ask, "What is important to you? What happens when you forget your homework? How do you feel about that? What are you learning from this experience? What ideas do you have to solve this problem (if he is interested in solving the problem)?" Otherwise, stick with empathy.

Another possibility is to do joint problem solving with him. Ask him what his goals are. Then ask him whether he would like to brainstorm *with* you to come up with a list of things that would help him achieve his goals. Then let him know you have faith in him to do what it takes to accomplish what he wants in life.

We would like to offer one more suggestion (even though you could do many other things to help your child feel empowered and encouraged): allow him to fail. Then show empathy and have faith in him to learn from his mistakes. One of the greatest lessons you can help your son learn is that his mistakes can be wonderful opportunities to learn and that he has the ability to recover and do better than ever because of his experience.

Healthy Homework Habits

Homework should be a child's responsibility, not a parent's, but it is worth repeating that children rarely love doing homework. If your goal is a young scholar who lives for spelling worksheets, you're likely to be sadly disappointed. Homework, when approached with kindness and firmness, can become an opportunity to teach children responsibility, self-discipline, and perhaps even a little reading, writing, and 'rithmetic.

Brandi is a bright nine-year-old and does moderately well in school, but she'd much rather be playing soccer or curling up with a good book every afternoon than doing her homework. Her teacher has sent notes home to Brandi's mom, Kathleen, telling her that Brandi's grades are suffering because her homework isn't being done adequately.

Kathleen believes education is important, but she knows her daughter well. Brandi is an active girl; sitting still for long periods of time is hard for her, and there are *so* many things she would rather be doing. Kathleen has already tried supervising the homework assignments; mother and daughter both wound up frustrated and irritated. So Kathleen invites Brandi to join her for a mini-family meeting to do some brainstorming about how to handle homework.

Kathleen and Brandi sit down together with lemonade and cookies on the appointed afternoon, Brandi looking a bit apprehensive because she already dreads the subject up for discussion.

"Your teacher tells me there's a bit of a problem with homework," Kathleen begins. Brandi immediately slumps her shoulders dramatically, sighs loudly, and rolls her eyes.

"Oh, Mom. Mrs. Peterson is such a drag. She has *no* imagination. All we do is the same old thing for homework, over and over. I hate it."

Kathleen laughs. "You sound like me at the same age. My fourth-grade teacher was pretty dull, too. I know homework bores you, especially when you'd rather be reading *Harry Potter.* But school is important, sweetie. What do you think we ought to do?"

Brandi shrugged and said, "I don't care." She wasn't in a hurry to help her mom with this one.

Kathleen gazed at her daughter for a moment. "Okay, let's try this. What sort of grades would be good enough for you?"

Brandi's forehead wrinkled—this had to be a trick question. "What do you mean, Mom?"

"Well, I know you're plenty smart. Look at how you love to read when you find a good book and how well you do on things you enjoy. I'm just wondering what grades would satisfy *you*. What would make you feel proud of yourself?"

Brandi hesitated, then, realizing her mother was serious, said, "I'd like to make B's, I guess. Sometimes A's are too hard for me, but I hate it when I get C's. And I know you and Dad aren't really happy with C's, either."

"We always love you, honey. But we do know you can do better. What if we aim for B's? That seems like a realistic goal. How well do you need to do on your homework to make B's?"

"I guess I could ask Mrs. Peterson that," Brandi said. "Would that really be enough? I've been thinking I had to make A's to make you happy, and it makes me feel so frustrated."

"I would be very happy with B's, Brandi," Kathleen said. "How about if we talk to Mrs. Peterson together?"

Armed with Mrs. Peterson's requirements for B's, Kathleen and Brandi drew up a new homework battle plan. Brandi would be in charge of gathering her supplies and doing the work; her mom would be able to ask occasionally how she was doing and what things she needed to finish. Brandi also admitted that taking time the night before to set her books and papers by the door helped her remember them in the morning without all the chaos. Brandi decided that it worked best for her to have an hour after school to herself to play soccer, read, or just relax and recover from the school day before settling down to tackle her homework assignments. She would then willingly do her homework. Mom and Brandi agreed to have another meeting in two weeks to see how things were going.

It took a couple of weeks and some minor adjustments to the plan before Kathleen and Brandi both felt the homework problem was being solved, but Brandi was very cooperative because she was respectfully included in the plans that affected her. One afternoon, Brandi came home waving a note from Mrs. Peterson complimenting her on the improvement in her work.

"I feel really good about this," Brandi said with a grin at her mom. "I guess I like doing better in school. I'm going out to play for a while, and then I have some math problems to do. See ya!"

Kathleen watched her daughter bounce out the door with a smile. It wasn't easy to keep the responsibility for Brandi's work where it belonged—with Brandi—but it certainly seemed to get good results.

Where Do We Go from Here?

Doing it "right" always looks easy in the pages of a book. It is considerably harder when you're faced with your own children and your expectations for them. There are dozens and dozens of parenting tools out there, all potentially successful. Your task as a parent is to know your children well, think long-term about what children are deciding and learning, and then make the best decisions you can. As we have discovered, good parenting is not always easy, nor does it always feel comfortable.

Take a moment to think yet again about your hopes and dreams for your children, about the character qualities you want them to develop and the people you hope they will become. Let your love for them—that overwhelming, heart-melting feeling you get at unexpected moments when they catch your eye, hug you, or simply lie dreaming on their pillows—empower you to choose life, strength, and competence for them. Love them enough to make the tough decisions: to teach, to guide, to let them wrestle a bit with life, and, in so doing, to learn how to live it well. Kind and firm parenting and long-range thinking will guide you along the way.

Conclusion

We have covered a lot of ground in these pages; you may be wondering where it all leads. Human beings usually find change a painful and challenging process, and the prospect of reexamining your beliefs about parenting, let alone actually changing them, may feel rather overwhelming. We understand; we've been there ourselves, and we continue to wrestle with our own changes and growth every time our children present us with a new issue, a new problem, or growth of their own. We have a sneaking suspicion that the process never really comes to an end.

The fact is that parents who love too much have a constant, unpleasant companion: worry. If you have been trying, knowingly or not, to control your children's beliefs and behavior, you probably worry about what they're doing. And if you pamper or rescue your children, we're willing to bet that in reflective moments, you wonder if it's really okay, if they're coming to the right conclusions about life. Parents who have discovered how to love their children in balanced, effective ways, who practice kind, firm parenting, and who can weigh the decisions their children are making worry, too—but they worry about different things.

There are no guarantees in giving birth to a baby, raising a child, and, eventually, releasing a young adult to live life on his or her own. All parents worry about illness and accidents, about wrong choices and mishaps, about the things other people may do that cause harm to the children we love so much.

> Most parents discover that in remembering cherished moments of life with children, they also connect with their truest self as parents.

Perhaps the biggest trap of loving too much is forgetting to simply enjoy your children—for who they are. Parents today have become obsessed with grades, performance, achievement ("Will my child get into a good college?"), and appearances—all in the name of love. But does this view make children feel loved? We don't think so. On a recent *Oprah* show, Toni Morrison suggested the best way to make your children feel loved. "Do your eyes light up when they enter your room?" she asked.

Learning to love children in healthy ways—to avoid the extremes we've spent so much time examining—allows parents to relax just a bit. Parents cannot guarantee that their children will never know pain or struggle. In fact, those things are among the few certainties in life.

But parents who have accepted the challenge to examine their beliefs and choices and who do their best to make decisions that use their hearts *and* their heads know that they have given their children the best possible chance of becoming capable, competent adults, the kind of people who can be truly happy and who can, in their own turn, love others, themselves, and eventually their own children in healthy ways.

You have both strengths and limitations; so do your children. Life will never be perfect for any of you, but it can be pretty wonderful. Close your eyes for a moment and let yourself see the faces of your children. Remember their first steps, their first words, their first explorations of their world. Most parents discover that in remembering those cherished moments of life with children, they also connect with their truest self as parents—the wisdom, the compassion, the courage, and the heart it takes to devote your time and energy to another human being. It is that indescribable feeling—the thing we call "love"—that gives you the power to make the everyday choices, some of them so difficult, that guide your children safely on their journey through life.

> Perhaps the biggest trap of loving too much is forgetting to enjoy your children for who they are.

If you have made it to the end of this book, you undoubtedly have questions. You must find—and trust—your own answers. You are the "expert" on your own children; we're just good at asking tough questions. Have you relied on excessive control or permissiveness?

Does it really work for you and your children? What are they learning about themselves and about life? Where will the decisions they are making lead them? And how do you stay connected enough to them to help them? The world we live in depends on the answers you—and all parents—find.

Index

Index • 313

Long-range results
excessive control, 33–34
importance, 44
knowledge of, 15–16
permissiveness, 33, 75–76
remembering, 25–26
Lott, Lynn, 242, 264, 294
Love
building blocks
dignity, 206–209
managing feelings, 216–217
mutual respect, 206–209
significant seven, 209–215
social interest, 215–216
understanding, 205–206
excessive, 3–12
guilt and, 106–107

M

Magic store technique,
102–103
Materialism
effects, 9–10
harm of, 24–25
pervasiveness, 16–18
Meal planning, 200, 201
Meetings. See Family meetings
The Millionaire Mind, 190
Mistakes, 187
Money
allowance
case study, 287–289
chores and, 290–293
starting, 285
as teaching tool, 285–287
managing, 282–285
spending, 281–282
stealing, 284–285
Morrision, Toni, 306
Mothers. See Working mothers
Mottoes, 197–200

Music, 267–269
Myths, parenting, 87–91

N

Needs
meeting, 221–222
prioritizing, 9
wants vs., 161–162
Neglect, 40–41
Neighbors, 101–103
Nelsen, Jane, 209
The Nurture Assumption: Why
Children Turn Out the
Way They Do, 227

O

Obesity, 77
On Becoming Babywise,
145–146
Oppositional defiant disorder,
55
Overprotection, 3–4

P

Pampering, 117, 305–306
Parenting
advice
adopting, 101
contradictory, 99–101
ignoring, 103–105
neighbors, 101–103
permissive advocates,
143–145
punishment advocates,
142–143, 145–147
attachment, 143–145
changes, adjustments, 120
decisions, 117
faith in, 276–277
frustrations, 279–280
goal, 278–279

About the Authors

 **Jane Nelsen** is a popular lecturer and coauthor of the entire POSITIVE DISCIPLINE series. She also wrote *From Here to Serenity: Four Principles for Understanding Who You Really Are.* She has appeared on *Oprah* and *Sally Jesse Raphael* and was the featured parent expert on the "National Parent Quiz," hosted by Ben Vereen. Jane is the mother of seven children and the grandmother of eighteen.

 **Cheryl Erwin** is a licensed marriage and family therapist in private practice, a lecturer and trainer, and the coauthor of four books in the POSITIVE DISCIPLINE series. Cheryl also has a weekly radio broadcast on parenting in the Reno, Nevada, area, where she lives with her husband and teenaged son.

For More Information

The authors provide dynamic lectures, seminars, and conference keynote presentations. In addition, workshops and facilitator training are scheduled throughout the United States each year. Workshops include:

Teaching Parenting the Positive Discipline Way
(a two-day workshop for parent educators)

Positive Discipline for Parents
(a one-day workshop)

Positive Discipline in the Classroom
(a one-day workshop for teachers and school personnel)

Dates and locations are available by contacting:

Empowering People
P.O. Box 1926
Orem, UT 84059
1-800-456-7770
Web site: www.positivediscipline.com

Order Form

To: Empowering People, P.O. Box 1926, Orem UT 84059
Phone: 1-800-456-7770 (credit card orders only)
Fax: 801-762-0022
Web site: www.positivediscipline.com for discount prices

BOOKS	Price	Quantity	Amount
Parents Who Love Too Much by Nelsen & Erwin	$16.95	_____	_____
Positive Time-Out by Nelsen	$12.00	_____	_____
Positive Discipline by Nelsen	$12.00	_____	_____
Raising Self-Reliant Children in a Self-Indulgent World by Glenn & Nelsen	$15.95	_____	_____
Positive Discipline: The First Three Years by Nelsen, Erwin, & Duffy	$16.00	_____	_____
Positive Discipline for Preschoolers by Nelsen, Erwin, & Duffy	$16.00	_____	_____
Positive Discipline for Teenagers by Nelsen & Lott	$16.95	_____	_____
Positive Discipline A–Z by Nelsen, Lott, & Glenn	$16.95	_____	_____
Positive Discipline for Single Parents by Nelsen, Erwin, & Delzer	$16.00	_____	_____
Positive Discipline for Your Stepfamily by Nelsen, Erwin, & Glenn	$16.95	_____	_____
Positive Discipline for Parenting in Recovery by Nelsen, Lott, & Intner	$12.95	_____	_____
Positive Discipline in the Classroom by Nelsen, Lott, & Glenn	$16.95	_____	_____
Positive Discipline: A Teacher's A–Z Guide by Nelsen, Duffy, Escobar, Ortolano, & Owen-Sohocki	$15.95	_____	_____
From Here to Serenity by Nelsen	$14.00	_____	_____

TAPES AND VIDEOS

	Price	Quantity	Amount
Positive Discipline cassette tape	$10.00	_____	_____
Positive Discipline video	$49.95	_____	_____
Building Healthy Self-Esteem Through Positive Discipline cassette tape	$10.00	_____	_____

SUBTOTAL _____

Sales tax: UT add 6.25%; CA add 7.25% _____

Shipping & handling: $3.00 plus $0.50 each item _____

TOTAL _____

(Prices subject to change without notice.)

METHOD OF PAYMENT (check one):
_____ Check made payable to Empowering People Books, Tapes, & Videos
_____ MasterCard, Visa, Discover Card, American Express

Card # _____ Expiration _____ / _____

Ship to _____

Address _____

City/State/Zip _____

Daytime phone _____ (_____) _____